Nicoletta Marini-Maio

A VERY SEDUCTIVE BODY POLITIC

Silvio Berlusconi in Cinema

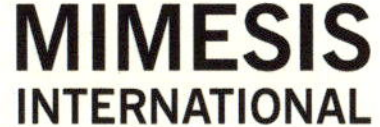

MIMESIS
INTERNATIONAL

Publication of this book was supported by a grant from Dickinson College

© 2015 – Mimesis International
www.mimesisinternational.com
e-mail: info@mimesisinternational.com
Book series: *Italian Frame*, n. 1
isbn 9788857526683
© MIM Edizioni Srl
P.I. C.F. 02419370305

TABLE OF CONTENTS

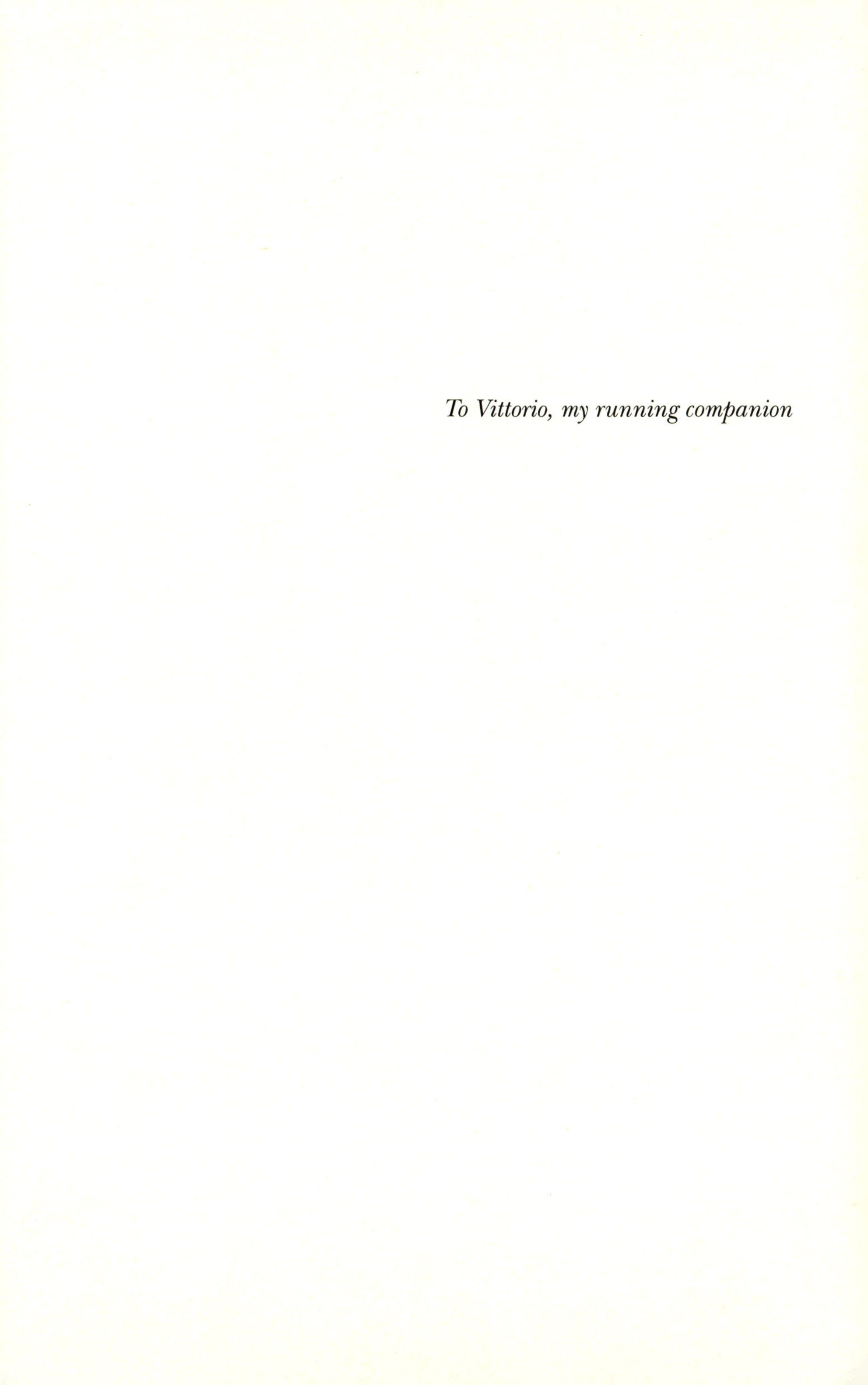

To Vittorio, my running companion

ACKNOWLEDGMENTS

I feel honored and humbled for authoring the inaugural volume of the *Italian Frame* series and am grateful to Christian Uva and Andrea Minuz for proposing my work to the publishing house and supporting me along the way. This book is the first tangible result of many readings, exchanges, discussions, and discoveries. The initial spur for my exploration of Berlusconi in cinema came from a roundtable on women and *Berlusconismo* held at the 2010 AAIS conference in Pittsburgh with my colleagues and dearest friends Paola Bonifazio, Giancarlo Lombardi and Ellen Nerenberg. I am indebted to all those who have helped me to devise this book in the subsequent years. Ellen and Paola were invaluable co-organizers of the 2012 Bologna conference 'Postfeminism? Culture, Politics, and Gender in the time of Berlusconi', which sparked great interest on the topic and motivated me to advance my research. In Bologna, I was fortunate to receive the academic support of Patrizia Violi, the warm reception of Annamaria Tagliavini, the generous sponsorship of Rita Finzi and the Coop, the skillful assistance of the smartest and most amiable graduate students I have ever met, Giuditta Bassano and Silvia Viti, and the delightful hospitality of my colleague and friend Sylvie Davidson.

As my work progressed, I had the privilege to entertain enlightening conversations with film directors Aurelio Grimaldi, Franco Maresco, and Roberta Torre, who kindly shared with me their thoughts and projects on Berlusconi. Although two current projects are either inaccessible (Grimaldi's) or unfinished (Torre's), I learned much from these directors and used their insights in this book. I am most appreciative of Ernest Ialongo, Chair of the 'Studies in Modern Italy Seminar' at Columbia University, for hosting a presentation of my project in March 2014. My superb respondent Silvia Carlorosi and all the seminar participants, including Catherine Proietto and Teresa Fiore, helped me to engage in a stimulating discussion that reverberates in this book. My presentation in the roundtable titled *Nuovo cinema politico*, organized by Christian Uva and Giancarlo Lombardi at the 2014 AAIS conference in Zurich, confirmed scholars' interest in the topic and fueled my motivation.

My deep gratitude goes to the Research and Development Committee at Dickinson College for funding my research and work on this book and to the Office of Global Study and Engagement for co-sponsoring the Bologna conference. There are others, less visible, that I would like to thank for inspiring me with precious input and invaluable support: Ida Dominijanni, Giancarlo Lombardi, Stefania Lucamante, Millicent (Penny) Marcus, and Colleen Ryan. I am thankful to my Dana Research Assistants Julia Barnes and Vivian Sicilia for their intellectual curiosity, and to all my students for encouraging me with their enthusiastic response to my work. I cannot adequately express my appreciation for the editorial intelligence and affectionate guidance of my dear friend Grace D'Alo. On a more personal note, I thank my sister Lorella, who inspired me with her tenacity in pursuing publication of her witty satire on Berlusconi, *I viaggi di Esse*. My children Costanza, who was also my generous reader, and Riccardo have always encouraged me, making me feel good about myself and this book. A special thanks goes to my running companion and partner in life, Vittorio, whose intellectual sharpness, zest for life, and reminders about healthy sleep habits make my life and work always enjoyable.

BERLUSCONISMO AND CINEMA

> *He was able to seduce the Italians like nobody else*
> *because he was much more Italian than Sordi.*
> *He was somewhat all of this together.*
> *Berlusconi is the anthropological, psychological,*
> *and philosophical representation of the Italian who already existed.*
>
> Franco Maresco

Why this book?

This book is an exploration of the cinematic dimensions of
'Berlusconismo' – as the time span from Berlusconi's decision to
enter politics since 1994 to date has been named. There is little
analysis of how Berlusconi's portrayal in film reflects, informs, or
questions his influence, and the discussion, although inspiring,
has focused almost exclusively on Nanni Moretti's *Il Caimano*.[1]
The reason for this void may be due to the fact that a number of
the films that center on Berlusconi are unknown to both the general public and scholars and a defined cinematic corpus has not
yet been delineated.[2] Ironically, there are few contemporary political leaders who have received more attention from cinema than
Silvio Berlusconi. Since Federico Fellini's *Ginger and Fred* in 1986,
more than thirty-three narrative or documentary films centering

---

1   In this regard, see the analyses by Clodagh Brook (2009), Silvia Carlorosi
    (2012), Roberto De Gaetano (2012), Christian Uva (2012), Pierpaolo
    Antonello (2013), Francesco Zucconi (2013), Chaterine O'Rawe (2014),
    and Giacono Tagliani (2014).
2   The cinematic corpus I propose is listed in the filmography at the end of
    this book. See also my article 'Before and After Silvio: A Corpus for Us
    All', in Giancarlo Lombardi and Christian Uva (forthcoming).

on Berlusconi — or evoking him in a substantial way — have been made, targeting national and international audiences. Currently, one more film by director Roberta Torre is in pre-production and presumably more will be made. Even for a political leader of his longevity, the proliferation of films about Berlusconi is unprecedented and this phenomenon invites attention. Across cultures, films on political leaders are increasing due to 'the over-mediatized nature of the contemporary political processes' (Brown, Vidal 2014:144), which captures public figures and events in different social contexts from those of their original occurrences and multiplies their semiosis. In fact, film reflects the mediated and collectively remembered images of political figures and historical events, expanding political leaders' lives and symbolic power beyond their original contexts (Zucconi 2009, Antonello 2009, Tagliani 2014). Contemporary examples include John F. Kennedy in *JFK* (1991), Elizabeth II in *The Queen* (2006), Tony Blair in the trilogy *The Deal* (2003), *The Queen* (2006), and *The Special Relationship* (2010), Idi Amin in *The Last King of Scotland* (2006), Richard Nixon and the Watergate scandal in *Frost/Nixon* (2008), George W. Bush in *W.* (2008), Giulio Andreotti in *Il Divo* (2008), Benito Mussolini in *Vincere* (2009), Margaret Thatcher in *The Iron Lady* (2011), and Martin Luther King Jr. in *Selma* (2014). More importantly, mediatization provides a platform that can paradoxically expand, criticize, and resist power (Antonello 2013: 164).

In this regard, the films on Silvio Berlusconi are emblematic as they cross an ample spectrum of dramaturgic possibilities and polysemic interpretations. According to categorizations of reception theory, the levels of 'polysemy' differ between texts (Fiske 1986, Condit 1991) because audiences are heterogeneous and their understanding of a film stems from their plural socio-cultural backgrounds. Leah Ceccarelli invites to a complex elaboration of the notion of polysemy. She indicates three primary types of polysemy:

– 'resistive reading', which pertains to the active interpretation of audiences that may confront mainstream discourses with a range of 'oppositional codes' (Hall 1980);

– 'strategic ambiguity', which defines an intentional ambiguous message of the text's creators addressing the expectations of a variety of viewers; and

– 'hermeneutic depth', which is the result of the critics' analytical interpretation of a text (1998).

In brief, the production of a wide horizon of meanings depends on the commercial, political, and cultural strategies of those who create the films — directors, screenwriters, producers — and on the diverse experiences, competencies, and predispositions of the communities that interpret them.[3] These processes of signification indicate that a singular, intrinsic meanings does not arise from a text; its meaning is created by the audiences' multiple ways of understanding it (Fish 1982: 168). In this sense, the appearance of Berlusconi in films is constructed as a polysemic image that lies in the eyes of the beholder. On the one hand, these films may appear as the result of an urge to explain, uncover, and denounce the hegemonic media and political power that Berlusconi incarnates. On the other hand, they reveal a strong fascination — almost an obsession — with *Il Cavaliere* (The Knight).[4] The 'interpretive communities' (Ibid.) that watch these films are therefore confronted with a number of choices: they can engage in processes of identification, jouissance (Barthes 1975), containment, spectralization, and opposition, depending on their own political and cultural background and on the filmmakers' strategic message.

The idea that propelled this study lies in the conviction that cinema can intercept the cultural configurations that Italian society has constructed of itself, the system(s) of power it has created, and its underlying symbols. Silvio Berlusconi's persona is an ideal vessel to explore these configurations insofar as it has iconic, indexical, and symbolic qualities (more on this later).[5] The analysis that this work proposes aims at pinpointing, clustering, and organizing concepts to identify the meanings assigned

---

3   For an innovative and complete overview of reception theories applied to Italian popular cinema from the economic boom to the 1970s, see Giacomo Manzoli (2013).

4   Silvio Berlusconi's nickname *Il Cavaliere* originates from the title of *Cavaliere del Lavoro* (Order of Merit for Labour) that former President of the Italian Republic, Giovanni Leone, awarded him in 1977. Berlusconi relinquished the title after being convicted of tax fraud in 2013 and banned from public office in May 2014 for two years.

5   The terms 'icon', 'index', and 'symbol' refer to Pierce's semiotic theory (The Peirce Edition Project, ed. 1998), pp. 291-92.

to these socio-cultural and political constructions. As Pierpaolo Antonello (2013: 160-67) points out, cinema reinterprets the past — even a very recent past — in a way that can interrogate 'the established structures of power (and of the shared image that we have of it)'. Berlusconi literally embodies such power and the 'shared image' that Italian society has of it. He has filled a central position in this society, hypnotizing both public discourse and individuals' subjectivities. He has achieved an unprecedented hegemonic role in the political, economic, and media spheres, while using a dumbfounding communicative style composed of flamboyant self-promotion, unbounded self-esteem, and spiteful condescension in matters of gender, sexuality, and ethnicity. Vincenzo Susca (Abruzzese, Susca 2004: 19) argues that Berlusconi has produced a semiotic 'fracasso' (fracas, ruckus) in the cultural and political system, to which the Italian public has responded with a high degree of 'rumore' (noise), around his persona. This *fracasso* has turned political debate in Italy into quarrelsome confrontation and has given Berlusconi a paramount position in all levels of society. Controversies swirl around his public and private life, from political corruption, tax evasion and fraud down to infringement of local building regulations. Almost every possible type of controversy or scandal regarding social practices, sexual habits, gender identity, immigration issues, ethnic integration, and euthanasia converge in Berlusconi's public performance. As the title of Abruzzese's and Susca's book paradoxically emphasizes, 'tutto è Berlusconi' (all is Berlusconi) in Italian society.

'All is Berlusconi' may sound extreme, but as Albertazzi and Rothenbergh (2009: 1) point out, 'it is difficult to overstate the influence of Silvio Berlusconi on contemporary Italian society, whether one is talking about its politics, culture or media industry.' His persona embodies the semiosis of a powerful icon, an index, and a symbol. His perennial smile, condescending attitude, cosmetic affectation, and sexual suggestiveness crystallize the iconic features of glamour and celebrity (Gundle 1995: 14-17; Belpoliti 2009). His persona serves as a precise index of historical and cultural parameters, political cachet, and socio-economic contexts. Finally, his persona symbolizes cultural myths and beliefs that have developed across time from

discourses on masculinity, sexuality, and contingent perceptions on 'italianità' (Italian-ness) and 'italiano medio' (Italian
everyman).[6]

Identifying and tracking the icons, indexes, and symbols that *Il
Cavaliere* incarnates, often takes one down unexpected paths. For
example, in 2001, with an Italian election in full swing, a study was
carried out on how advanced dementia affected a sixty-six year old
Italian house wife who displayed 'an extremely severe deficit in the
recognition of faces' (Mondini, Semenza 2006). The report, titled
'How Berlusconi Keeps His Face: A Neuropsychological Study in
a Case of Semantic Dementia', discusses how this patient was unable to identify even the faces most familiar to her, including her
husband's and children's, but consistently recognized a picture
of Berlusconi and named him (332). When asked about who Berlusconi was, she gave basic but correct information: she said that
he was a wealthy man, a television owner, and a politician. Pho-
tographs of several different people of varying relationship and
familiarity were shown to the woman on several occasions. Other
than Berlusconi, the only images that the woman recognized were
those of Christ on the cross and a person she simply called 'the
Pope', although she could not recognize him without his paraphernalia (334). The two scientists who conducted the research
state that the effect of Mr. Berlusconi's 'pervasive propaganda' is
unprecedented in neuropsychological literature and conclude
that Berlusconi's face was seen as an icon rather than a face (332).

Ten years later, in the online edition of national newspaper *Corriere della Sera,* a reader posted this comment on journalist Beppe
Severgnini's blog 'Italians': 'I am thirty-four and grew up mod-
eling my expectations on the products of the immense dream
factory created by the companies that he founded and that his
family today firmly controls. Whether I like it or not, I "am" Silvio
Berlusconi as well' (Lombardi 2012).[7] This comment illustrates

---

6   For an analysis of the discourses on *Italiano medio* in Comedy Italian
     Style, see Vittorio Spinazzola (1985), Goffredo Fofi (2004), Sergio
     Rigoletto (2007) and Silvana Patriarca (2010). A discussion of how
     cinematic construct of Italian everyman is inscribed in Silvio Berlusconi's
     communicative strategies is in this book, pp. 29-39.
7   All the original extracts from Italian texts or films quoted in this book are
     my own traslation.

the intimate relationship that the young man internalizes between himself, Berlusconi's media system and Berlusconi's body. In a subdued confessional tone, he maintains that he formed his heuristic framework on the cultural models offered by Berlusconi's media empire and that his own self contains — is — Silvio Berlusconi, too. The Berlusconi in his comment is obviously not a corporeal entity in flesh and blood, but the metonymical body of the 'immense dream factory' that Berlusconi created and 'firmly controls'. In other words, he perceives Berlusconi's body as a semiotic repository of the feelings, perceptions, perspectives, experiences, beliefs, desires, and knowledge that create subjectivity.

The case of the dementia patient and the young man's reflection on his relationship with Berlusconi's 'dream factory' are isolated but compelling indicators of Silvio Berlusconi's pervasive influence on how Italians may relate to his figure. Individuals construct and negotiate who they are and how they are positioned in the world based on a number of internal and external factors — ideological, political, sexual, technological, historical, relational, cultural, to say the least — but Berlusconi's persona may be perceived as the predominant force that determines subjectivities. In fact, in twenty years, Berlusconi has become a 'myth of mass' and exerted a mesmerizing effect on public discourse, cultural perceptions, and representations (Abruzzese, Susca 2004: 73; Dei 2011: 471). Despite his political downfalls in 1996 and 2006, his role in the deterioration of Italy's political profile internationally, his numerous trials and alleged crimes, his controversial resignation in 2011, his conviction for fiscal fraud in 2013, and his consequent removal from Parliament in 2014, Berlusconi's mediated image and words continue to excite, entertain, and inflame not only his electorate, but also his political opponents and all the social actors.[8]

---

8   Silvio Berlusconi has been tried for corruption of judges, infringement of antitrust laws, drug traffic, bribery, complicity in massacre, bribery of senators, association with the Mafia and money-laundering, abuse of power, defamation, prostitution of minors, and fiscal evasion and fraud. A brief summary of Berlusconi's political history is in the appendix of this book. For a synthetic overview of Berlusconi's political and legal trajectories, see Claudia Mariotti (2011), Alessandro Chiaramonte and Roberto D'Alimonte (2012), and the dossier of *La Repubblica* (2015). The talk of the *discesa in campo* is accessible in *Corriere della Sera* (1994).

During the writing of this book, Berlusconi was often at the center of political controversy. In July 2014, his conviction for prostitution of minors was overturned and in March 2015, the acquittal was upheld. The backdrop to these charges and attendant legal processes is as follows. In 2013, Berlusconi was sentenced to seven years of detention for charges stemming from an alleged sex-for-hire affair with Karima El Mahroug, a Moroccan youg woman known as 'Ruby Rubacuori' (Ruby the Heart Stealer) when she was a minor. Ruby was detained on charges of theft and Berlusconi was also implicated for abusing his office for placing pressure on the head of the police to release her. Berlusconi claimed that Ruby was related to former President Hosni Mubarak of Egypt, and suggested that her arrest could cause a diplomatic incident (Squire 2011; Polovedo 2014).

Since his most recent appellate exculpation, there has been a frantic and hyperbolic discussion of Berlusconi's return to center stage of Italian politics. For example, Giovanni Orsina (2014) speaks of a 'coup de théâtre' and examines how Berlusconi's return may influence the right-wing party's options and ability to play an effective role in the current political landscape. Giuseppe Alberto Falci (2014) discusses Berlusconi's temptation to rejoin the moderate group that split from his party in 2013 and accordingly align himself with the current democratic majority. Alexander Stille (2014) compares Berlusconi's 2011 resignation to the end of Cold War, although on a smaller scale, and maintains that his return might severely hinder the current Prime Minister's, Matteo Renzi, efforts to reform Italy and the positive momentum toward that reform since 2013. In fact, Berlusconi's ability to revamp his political persona, both nationally and internationally, has been going on since 2008 and has refueled his return to center stage. In 'The Mummy Returns', Frank Bruni of *The New York Times* cites several titles from the international press alluding to the question of the return and wonders whether Berlusconi is going to 'feed yet another time, more zombie than mummy, on Italy's body politic' (2013).

This book investigates how cinema can set aside this *fracasso* and deconstruct this leader's omnipotent and pervasive image. Cinema, I argue, deciphers this indistinct wholeness — the *tutto* — while complicating the relationship between fiction, archive, historical narrative, and cultural discourse (O'Leary 2011). Cinema traces new correlations and challenges the established perceptions of Berlusconi that have permeated contemporary society. This analysis is even more urgent if one considers that a great number of the films that this volume discusses have encountered enormous distribution difficulties. A few of them have been released in a few theaters, but only for a very limited time — in certain cases for no more than one day or two. Some films have endured a particularly difficult destiny: Nanni Moretti's *Il Caimano* (2006), for example, appeared on television only five years after its original release in theaters. Aurelio Grimaldi's *Il più migliore al mondo* (2001), produced on DVD, was not accepted by Italian retailers, and made a very brief appearance in France. It resurfaced on television in 2005, but is now impossible to find.[9] Finally, some films were never distributed in Italy, and even if they are now accessible on DVD or on the web, most are still unknown to the general public. Mapping all these films in a coherent, intelligible corpus is a way to bring back to life existent but often invisible perspectives and contextualize their political and cultural interpretations. To some extent, Berlusconi's *fracasso* thrives as long as thoughtful, in-depth and comprehensive review is impeded by censorship of randomly oppositional viewpoints.

A Very Seductive Body Politic

A fundamental concern in the films on Berlusconi is the representation of the leader's body as the intersection of physical and symbolic features. As Ernst H. Kantorowicz (1957) describes in his seminal book *The King's Two Bodies*, the sovereign's body is endowed with a double nature, that is, the material body and the mystic body (i.e., its rituals and liturgies), which is where the royal power enacts itself and acquires its significations. The contemporary mediated 'society of the spectacle' (Debord 1967) translates

---

9   Director Aurelio Grimaldi and producer Leonardo Giuliano do not have a full copy of the film. They kindly tried to provide me one through *La7*, the TV network where the film was broadcast, but with no success (personal communication). See also this book, chapter 4, p. 78.

the idea of the 'king's two bodies' into another form of duplicity, consisting of the simultaneous presence of the body's materiality and its spectacularization in the public sphere (Zucconi 2009). This applies to all political leaders. In films centering on political figures, the actorial efforts to recreate the leader's body and features of sovereignty are often more important than the plot itself (Antonello 2013: 164). The actual leaders' physical traits, which the audience perceives as both iconic and familiar, receive new political dimensions from the actor (Ibid.). With the passage of time, the actorial masks tend to overlap and sometimes overtake the real faces of political leaders.[10] In certain cases actors make historical figures more vulnerable and retrospectively challenge the abstract nature of the power they incarnate. For example, Hitler has acquired a more human, fragile quality thanks to Bruno Ganz's melancholic gaze in *Downfall* (2004); for the spectator, Mahatma Gandhi is one with Ben Kingsley's benevolent portrayal in *Gandhi* (1982); Che Guevara is fiercer in the interpretation by Benicio Del Toro in *Che* (2008); Giulio Andreotti is engraved with an unforgettable Machiavellian aura by virtue of Tony Servillo's performance in *Il Divo* (2008); and Abraham Lincoln is endowed with the qualities of a thoughtful father and considerate husband as acted by Daniel Day-Lewis's in *Lincoln* (2013).

What happens in the representation of Berlusconi's body? Which new political dimensions, challenges, and face(s) does cinema assign to him? To what extent do these faces replicate or conflict with the mediated ones? In which ways can the viewers engage with these processes of representation? Attempting to answer these questions has been the most fascinating and burdensome part of this investigation because of the polysemy of Berlusconi's body and the heterogeneity of the cinematic corpus. In film, Berlusconi's body is represented in a number of ways: as a disembodied figure in *Il Caimano* (The Caiman, 2006), as an allegory of pleasure in *Viva la libertà* (Long Live Liberty, 2013), as a Kurtz-Brando metaphor in *Shooting Silvio* (2006), as an ex-

---

10   Roberto De Gaetano discussed in depth the idea of the crystallization of the political leader's face into a mask. With regard to Nanni Moretti's *Il caimano* (The Caiman), De Gaetano argues that Moretti replaces Berlusconi's mask — as depicted by the media — with his own actorial mask (2012, 'Parte Quarta', Kindle ebook).

pressionless puppet in *Ops… Ho ammazzato Berlusconi!* (Oops… I Killed Berlusconi, 2008), as a trigger for political self-reflection in *Arance e martello* (Oranges and Hammer, 2014), as a symbolic presence in *Sorelle d'Italia* (Sisters of Italy, 2010), as a well-connected Mafia member in *La Trattativa* (State-Mafia Pact, 2014), and as a catalyst of existential failure in *Belluscone. Una storia siciliana* (Belluscone. A Sicilian Story, 2014). Even Berlusconi's mediated image has acquired unforeseen symbolic meanings, as seen in Berlusconi's spectral image of power in *La bella addormentata* (Dormant Beauty, 2012), or in the self-referential icons of *Silvio Forever* (2011). This is only a partial list, but it is emblematic of the ways in which cinema captures and questions the tension between Berlusconi's body and the meanings that we, the 'interpretive communities' (Fish 1982: 168), produce and assign to it. These films explore complex symbolic spaces in which cultural traditions, sense of belonging, desires, and existential objectives shift.

In working to represent Berlusconi's body, cinema also deconstructs the sophisticated communicative strategy that Berlusconi uses to endow his body with seductive features in the mediated sphere (Belpoliti 2009; Gundle 1995: 14-17). Berlusconi stages his material body as a prothesis of the televisual body and proposes his persona as the one among many, the everyman and bearer of the 'national character' (Patriarca 2010: 268-69), who can seduce the audience by presenting himself as its natural interface. He offers a sort of communion, one which is certainly lay and mundane, but endowed with ritualistic signifiers. Between his body and the people comprising the TV audience are liturgies and practices that, before Berlusconi's *discesa in campo* (descent into the field), were at the margins of the political discourse. The public performance of his persona calls upon people, the so-called *italiano medio* (Italian everyman) population, to desire him as their leader, to share his feelings, and identify with the Italian everyman par excellence. Susca claims that Berlusconi has constructed himself as 'a phantasmatic body, on which the collective imagination projects its most intimate desires, it is an oneiric mirror in which the Hollywoodians — in their late televisual version — see their dreams to materialize and become true.' (2004: 99)

Susca's perspective, partially shared by Bobbio (2008), Ricci (2003) and Lazar (2009), is problematic because, as Dei (211: 476) argues, it considers both spectators and electors as 'passive receptors of marketing strategies'. Dei (474) suggests that Berlusconi's message reaches the electorate because he strategically blends categories of high and low, popular and elitist, informal and institutional, personal and public, and other polarities that characterize modern socio-cultural spheres. Constructing his image according to this multiple semiosis strategically positions Berlusconi as omnipresent. It is crucial to highlight that in the construction of this strategic message, the political, mediated, and symbolic discourses overlap and the intellectuals who were supposed to mediate between dominant classes and popular masses — according to an orthodox Gramscian theory — are not needed anymore. In other words, Berlusconi's body makes an ample part of the electorate's perceived needs and desires visible and accessible. The admiration and empathy propelled by this representation derive from a process of self-projection and self-recognition (Ginsborg 2004: 107-112), which does not need intermediary figures or mediations. In addition, Berlusconi has loaded both his persona and his political victories with metaphors of success and consequently increased the sense of power that his body emanates. He has done what a sovereign does: using prostheses to expand his body, endowing it with 'symbolic and operative value' (Abruzzese, Susca 2004: 15). In so doing, he has transformed his body into a sort of collective simulacrum (Ibid.), which invites identification as a grandiose and powerful version of a shared idea of Italian-ness.

In a rich essay on 'charisma and manufactured charisma', Stephen Gundle (1998: 181) reminds us that Nietzsche and Weber indicate in the 'erotic orgy' the 'technique for simulation of the charismatic moment' and in 'sexual exuberance' one of the primary characteristics of charisma'. He argues that, although mass culture does not inevitably lead to charisma in public figures, Berlusconi 'manufactured' charisma by appropriating the 'language of glamour' and its attributes, such as 'wealth, beauty, euphoric happiness, sex appeal, vanity' (185). As Marco Belpoliti (2009: 49) maintains, a great deal of Berlusconi's fascination to Italian political constituencies stems from the strong sexual vibrations that the leader's body emanates and his public performance is based on the meticulous construction of a seductive body. Susca claims that it is necessary to understand

> the erotic and religious character of Berlusconian leadership [...]. Berlusconi confirms the truthfulness of this perspective and adds a personal trait to it: he also becomes a *stimulator* of the audience and a dispenser/distributor of passion, warmth, entertainment and pleasure. He combines in his body the mythical figures of the god and prostitute (Abruzzese, Susca 2004: 90-91).[11]

This performative and strategic 'presentation of self' (Goffman 1959) could not prevent or erase oppositional discourses and cultures from the cultural horizon. Quite the contrary: the 'semiotic excess' (Fiske 1986: 403) that pervades the significations of Berlusconi's mediated body solicits dissent and resistance. The idea of semiotic excess is that mediated communication consists of an associative, non logic proliferation of segments that go 'beyond narrative' (402) and pertain to different semiotic codes. The 'fissures' that remain open because of the absence of a narrative, closed structure allow 'ideologically contradictory readings' (Ibid.). Fiske claims that 'once the ideological hegemonic work has been performed, there is still excess meaning that escapes the control of the dominant and is thus available for the culturally subordinate to use for their own cultural-political interests' (403). In other words, when meanings proposed by mediated processes conflict with viewers' beliefs, the possibility for oppositional discourse arises.[12]

Beyond doubt, there have been powerful oppositional discourses to Berlusconi, especially — but not only — among intellectual circles and left-wingers. In fact, since his 'descent into the field' in 1994, political debate has centered almost exclusively on the *Berlusconismo* / anti-*Berlusconismo* dyad. Associations, journal-

---

11 With regard to the feminization of Berlusconi's body, see Catherine O'Rawe's warning on the risk to 'collapse into its degraded and abject other, femininity, in a way that clearly seeks to shore up and maintain gender distinctions' (5).

12 For an informative analysis of Berlusconi's polarizing effect on Italian constituencies, arousing both positive and hostile reactions, see Agnew (2011).

ists, writers, filmmakers, activists, and grass root movements have challenged Berlusconi on many fronts and the electorate voted him out of office in 2006 (Albertazzi, Brook, Ross, Rothenbergh 2009). However, thanks to the man's ability to create consensus around the symbolic configurations of his body, Berlusconi — as a metaphor for the national body politic — has repeatedly overcome the strategies of resistance and dissent emerging from the Italian political arena during his cultural and political hegemony. In fact, as Albertazzi and Rothenberg (10) point out, Berlusconi embraces the Foucaldian notion of power as a 'complex strategical situation' and a 'multiplicity of force relations' (Foucault 1979: 92-7) insofar as he has skillfully manipulated the political divisions of his opponents and gained favor by delegitimizing them and making them appear as a radical minority detached from the real problems of the country.

Pierpaolo Antonello claims that cinema is 'the great system apt to reveal the anthropological structures that cross unconsciously or as subtexts the modern imaginary' (2013: 166-67). In fact, cinema has captured the deep friction between the seduction that Berlusconi's body exerts and the opposition it raises. Most of the narrative and documentary films on Berlusconi focus on the dialectic between conflicting discourses of power. There are many examples: the connections between politics and media, the conflicting images of Berlusconi as a successful self-made man and a corrupt individual hand in glove with the Mafia (according to a conspiracy plot that is typical of the genre), the clash between diverse political cultures, the changes in models of leadership and the parallelism between *Berlusconismo* and Fascism, the desire for or rejection of models of consumption, and the tension between heteronormative and postfeminist ideas of gender, among others.

Where to Start from: Berlusconismo *before Berlusconi*

A number of scholars, historians, and journalists have explored the category of *Berlusconismo* from a variety of theoretical perspectives. The very first analysis is Norberto Bobbio's (2008) bitter reflection on the arc of *Berlusconismo* from 1994 to 2008. It exemplifies the left-wing intellectuals' surprise for and philosophical distance from an unpredictable and perversely modern political phenomenon produced by mediatization and populistic slogans. Comprehensive exegeses of *Berlusconismo* and Berlusconi's media empire, patrimony, and alleged relationship with the Mafia have been published. Some claim this relationship gave Berlusconi the financial means to start his lightning career in the early 1980s (Stille 2006; Travaglio, Veltri 2001). According to this perspective, Berlusconi is a cultural and political anomaly in the Italian and international context, which should be challenged by legal means, but should also be seen against the backdrop of mass culture and postmodernity. Along this line, Paul Ginsborg and Enrica Asquer (2011) provided the first overarching vision of *Berlusconismo* as a power system shaped by historical, sociological, and economic factors as well as cultural and discursive practices. Along with Ginsborg and Asquer (2011) Antonio Gibelli (2010) emphasizes the changes of mentality, aspirations, and desires that occurred after the economic boom and the student movement of the 1960s, and the more recent change in the international political scenario following the collapse of Communism in 1989. Other studies ascribe *Berlusconismo* as socioeconomic and cultural paradigms identified in Edward Banfield's seminal work on the 'backwardness' and 'amoral familism' of Italian society (Banfield 1958; Mancino, Galli Della Loggia 1998: 87; Mancini 2011: 50). Several philosophical studies center on the notion of populism and link it to the cultural and economic coordinates that are at the core of Berlusconi's system of power (Genovese 2011). Within the framework of feminist theory, Ida Dominijanni's study is illuminating as it identifies and deconstructs the symbolic processes enacted by the 'regime of enjoyment' embodied by Berlusconi (2014). In particular, Dominijanni's work sheds light on the relationhips between money, sexuality, and politics in *Berlusconismo* and offers a deeply critical analysis that includes cultural and cinematic products.

A solid perspective on *Berlusconismo* is Giovanni Orsina's historical analysis (2013). Projecting it onto a logic of *long durée*, Orsina sees *Berlusconismo* as a complex phenomenon that may have roots in the *Risorgimento*, the turbulent period between the Congress of Vienna in 1815 and the crowning of the first King of Italy in 1861, leading to Italy's unification. Orsina claims that *Berlusconismo* is the upshot of a historical trajectory that starts in the nineteenth century with the failure of the moderate right. This failure led to Fascism in the 1920s. Fascism effectively eliminated the development of a modern conservative party in Italy and resulted in a long hegemony of an 'orthopedic' and 'pedagogical' left wing in postwar Italy.[13]

Because of the surplus of meanings assigned to Berlusconi's figure by the texts and practices circulating in Italian society — mediated images, cultural and linguistic habits, ideas of power, ways to create consensus, and heteronormative concepts of femininity and masculinity, to mention only a few — this study favors a horizon of analysis that crosses both chronological and generic boundaries. My investigation is based on the belief that, in line with the concept of 'postmodern *impegno*' (engagement) theorized by Pierpaolo Antonello and Florian Mussgnug (2009: 4), an analysis of cinema as a cultural product should not be limited by 'any restrictive ideological brace' (11). Therefore, the cinematic corpus that my study proposes is not restricted to those films that one could conventionally consider *impegnati* (engaged), such as biopics, documentaries and narrative film *di denuncia* (of denunciation), and satires. This corpus includes also several popular movies produced to entertain a large public, a few films which do not focus mainly on Berlusconi but patently evoke his persona to signify a cultural context, and even *Viva la libertà* (Long Live Liberty, 2013), a film in which Silvio Berlusconi cannot be historically identified according to a naturalistic register of representation but is nonetheless powerfully foreshadowed. As Orsina goes back to Risorgimento to examine the original roots of *Berlusconismo*, my exploration of Berlusconi in cinema begins before Berlusconi entered the public stage, with the *commedia all'italiana* (comedy Italian style) sub-genre. The first film discussed is *La più bella serata della mia vita* (The Most Wonderful Evening of My Life, 1972), directed by Ettore Scola. In this film, a proto-type Berlusconi figure foreshadows the converging cultural and political

---

13   For the linkage with Fascism, see also Gianpasquale Santomassimo (2005) and the two collections of essays 'Berlusconismo e Fascismo' (1) (January 2011) and 'Berlusconismo e Fascismo' (2) (February 2011).

dimensions signifying Berlusconi's emergence. My analysis ends with the discussion of Guido Bianchi's *Arance e Martello* (Oranges and Hammer, 2014) and the announcement of a film that is currently in pre-production: Roberta Torre's *La caduta dell'impero* (The Collapse of the Empire).

The corpus discussed within resists rigid categorization and highlights 'openness' in response to a cinema that continues to question its object of representation — Berlusconi's body — and produce new meanings. Tracing *Berlusconismo* back to its tragicomic cinematic prototype is a means to single out and deconstruct a communicative strategy based on cinematic constructs — the Italian everyman, Italian-ness, and the 'national character' (Patriarca 2010: 266) — circulating in Italian society before Berlusconi emerged. When he 'entered the field', he embodied and validated his political project in an immediately comprehensible and shared language and set of cultural symbols.

The corpus

Cinema hones in on Berlusconi's appeal and sexual connotations. A number of films focus on his body from different perspectives, in a variety of genres, and across time. For readability and focus, this book does not attempt an in-depth analysis of all the feature films relating to Berlusconi. My study is rather an exploration of a heterogeneous corpus that I organize and cluster according to pertinent thematic, stylistic, or generic relationships. In other words, I propose a map of the representations of Berlusconi in cinema as a meaningful way to navigate *Berlusconismo.* This means that my exploration uncovers not only the historical persona, but also a pervasive semiotic category that intersects cultural and political contexts across time, in which the recent history of the country is inscribed and Italian society mirrors itself. To quote Susca again, 'the character represents for us an extraordinary pre-text to make sense of our past and future history' (Abruzzese, Susca: 149).

After this preliminary consideration of the pervasiveness of *Berlusconismo* and its discursive practices, the book discusses the corpus of films on Berlusconi in five chapters. The first chapter, 'The *italiano medio:* Prefiguring Berlusconi', highlights traits of the *commedia all'italiana* (Comedy Italian Style) from the pre-Berlusconi era. In these films, the depiction of the *italiano medio* (Italian everyman) articulated a cynical national self-image, setting the stage for the popularization of the cultural icons and consumerist codes of *Berlusconismo.* The critical focus of this section is *La più bella serata della mia vita* (The Most Wonderful Evening of My Life, 1972), by Ettore Scola. This is a black comedy staging a mock trial against a proto-Berlusconian parvenu, the entrepreneur Alfredo Rossi (Alberto Sordi).

The second chapter 'Shifting bodies: Estranged Representations' centers on *Ginger e Fred* (1986), by Federico Fellini, *Il Caimano* (The Caiman, 2006), by Nanni Moretti, *La bella addormentata* (Dormant Beauty, 2012), by Marco Bellocchio, and *Viva la libertà* (Long Live Liberty, 2013), by Roberto Andò. It discusses the conflicting relationship between politics and the media from both a narrative and figurative standpoint. It focuses on the appearances of Berlusconi's body, including the real Berlusconi from the archival footage, and centers on the four directors' estranged impersonations of Berlusconi as a symbolic and spectral body.

In the third chapter, 'Berlusconi *in morte*: Killing the King's Body', three narrative films staging the killing of Berlusconi are discussed, namely: *Bye Bye Berlusconi* (2005), by Jan Henrik Stahilberg, *Shooting Silvio* (2007), by Berardo Carboni, and *Ops... Ho ammazzato Berlusconi!* (Oops... I Killed Berlusconi, 2008), by Gianluca Rossi and Daniele Giometto. This chapter discusses how the semiotic excess of Berlusconi's body — 'all is Berlusconi', Abruzzese and Susca remind us — erases the apparent disproportion between the protagonists' existential or political motivations and the assassination of the epitome of the *italiano medio.*

The fourth chapter is titled 'The non-fictional body politic'. It briefly presents a selection of documentaries focusing on Berlusconi's parable, or the Italy of *Berlusconismo,* including *Quando c'era Silvio* (When There Was Silvio, 2005), by Beppe Cremagnani and Enrico Deaglio, *Silvio Forever* (2011), by Roberto Faenza and Filippo Macelloni, and *S.B. Io lo conoscevo bene* (S.B. I Knew Him Well, 2012), by Giacomo Durzi and Giovanni Fasanella. These documentaries explore the figure of Silvio Berlusconi through a great variety of non-fictional modalities, offering different, often conflicting perspectives on Berlusconi's theatrical, constructed, and mediated body. In this chapter a few films made primarily for international audiences are also briefly presented: *Sua Maestà Silvio Berlusconi* (His Majesty, Silvio Berlusconi, 2003), by Stéphane Bentura, *Citizen Berlusconi* (2003), by Andrea Cairola and Susan Gray, and *Berlusconi, Affaire Mondadori* (2006), by Mosco Boucault.

The fifth and last chapter 'Berlusconi *post-mortem*' discusses two recent films on the aftermath of *Berlusconismo,* namely: *Belluscone. Una storia siciliana* (Belluscone. A Sicilian Story, 2014) by Franco Maresco, and *Arance e Martello* (Oranges and Hammer, 2014), by Diego Bianchi. It includes excerpts from my interview of director Maresco.

Italian society is genuinely dumbfounded by Berlusconi. This book scrutinizes the roots, impact and aftermath of this astonishment through the prism of cinema. Seen from this perspective, *Berlusconismo* does not appear anymore as an unwieldy body of speculations, theories, and analyses that cannot be reconciled into one coherent explanation. The dark room shuts down the *fracasso* and illuminates the idiosyncratic intersection of political, cultural, and economic forces that emerges through Berlusconi's seductive body politic.

1.
THE *ITALIANO MEDIO*: PREFIGURING BERLUSCONI

It's not the Berlusconi in him that I fear, it's the Berlusconi in me.
Giorgio Gaber

Silvio as the italiano medio*: A Biopolitical Project*

In an entertaining piece on the concept of 'moral degradation' as the basic feature of highbrow Italian cinema, Andrea Minuz (2014: 190) asks rhetorically: 'Where does moral degradation come from? You can't be wrong, moral degradation begins in 1994.' That year marks Berlusconi's cataclysmic 'descent into the field', which shook the Italian political arena and changed its communication standards. The target of Minuz's irony is the idea that Berlusconi's political occupation indicated the emergence of an intrinsically amoral '*anthropological bloc*' in Italy (Genovese 2011: 37. Emphasis is in the text). Genovese argues that this *bloc* was engrained within Italian society long before Berlusconi's appearance and that it is comprised of people who are both 'actors and passive subjects' of the new political scene (Ibid.). He claims that they are mainly preoccupied with their 'particulare' (self-interest), have evaded taxes 'always and as much as possible', and expect politicians to protect 'the petty cares in their lives' (Ibid.).[1] However, as Barra and Scaglioni (2013), Dominijanni (2014a) and Ortoleva (1995) emphasize, the complicated cultural and sociological changes that have occurred in Italy in the last twenty years must be understood within a more complex and broader framework that needs to take into account the national

---

1   By using the word 'particulare', Genovese is referring to the proverbial definition by Renaissance historian Francesco Giucciardini (1576), who praised self-interest as a quality for personal and social success.

and international 'cultural and media dynamics' (Scaglioni 2013: 79).[2]

Surely, Berlusconi's position of power as both a media tycoon and political leader solicited processes of 'mainstreaming' (Gerbner 1998: 183-4) in the electorate. In fact, the heavy exposition of viewers to commercial networks, the effects of mediatization on many aspects of everyday life, and the advent of 'pop-politics' (Dei 2011) had a strong impact on societal changes and political leadership. However, until the 1980s, the pedagogical model of 'public service' (Scaglioni 2015: 7) had been a monopoly of the three Italian main parties — the Christian Democrats, the Socialists, and the Communists — that controlled, respectively, the three public national channels: RAI 1, 2, and 3. The transformation from paleo- to neotelevision (Williams 1974, Eco 1983) ended that monopoly, addressed the viewers' demands for entertainment (Barra and Scaglioni 2013: 80-86), and changed not only the practices of consumption but also the idea of television itself.

The aggressive strategy that Berlusconi devised to pursue his political and economic project included the narrative and symbolic use of his own body. Silvana Patriarca points out that his persona has been linked to the stereotypical elements of what is perceived as the Italians' 'national character' (266), or the *italiano medio* (Italian everyman). In fact, he has used his own persona to occupy the Italian public stage with a grotesque 'hedonistic body' that is deeply rooted 'within the nation's autobiography and collective imaginary' (Dominijanni 2014a: 19). Both his appeal as the epitome of the 'national character' and the strategic message that emanates from it have been perceived as a conglomerate of ideas, experiences, contexts, and lifestyles that public opinion is largely willing to recognize and embrace as its own. In other words, Berlusconi has deliberately created a public performance of his own self that overlaps with the construct of the *italiano medio*, and this has consequently affected the electorate's reactions to his political agenda. This junction between his performance and

---

2   Pier Paolo Pasolini, Italian film director and writer, first denounced the 'antropological mutation' that was taking place in Italy in the 1970s, leading Italian society to cultural and social homologation (1999). In Pasolini's view, consumerism and television were to blame for this change.

the paradigm of the Italian 'national character' creates parallels between Berlusconi's body and that of Alberto Sordi, the corrupt and immature Italian everyman character in *commedia all'italiana* (Comedy Italian Style). This sub-genre constituted a series of films produced in Italy between postwar and the late 1970s. However, while Sordi can be interpreted as a proto-Berlusconi figure, this does not mean that we should consider *Berlusconismo* as the culmination of Italians' democratic immaturity and natural propensity to corruption (Albertazzi and Rothenberg 2009: 10). It is quite the opposite. As Ida Dominijanni maintains,

> while it is not simple to capture the mix of political and biopolitical ingredients that enabled Berlusconi to gain such deep entrenchment in Italian society, it is a mistake to reduce such ingredients to a mix of folklore, illegality, and media manipulation, which often has been the most common assessment of this situation both in Italy and abroad (2014b: 170).

The biopolitical project devised through Berlusconi's body and *Berlusconismo* incorporated symbols of popular culture that had been circulating for some time. A number of cinematic productions foreshadow the figure of Berlusconi *before* the real one actually entered the public stage. In this chapter, through the case study of Ettore Scola's *La più bella serata della mia vita* (The Most Wonderful Evening of My Life, 1972), I argue that the chronotype of the *italiano medio* — a central element of the 1970s Comedy Italian Style — is in fact a rudimentary proto-Berlusconi figure. The *italiano medio* is a crystallized cultural symbol and Italian society has contributed to its production, embodiment, and sanctioning within the Comedy Italian Style. Combining the comic and the tragic, the films in this sub-genre employed 'a cynical sense of humor reflecting the human drive for survival in the face of overwhelming obstacles [...] [and] almost always included an undercurrent social malaise' (Bondanella 2009: 181).

Besides the films' often controversial themes and tragicomic plots, the most noteworthy feature of this sub-genre is the male protagonist, or the *italiano medio*. According to Vittorio Spinazzola, the *italiano medio* represents certain shared values and experiences that the 'average' Italian viewer perceives as normal

(1985: 289). In his analysis of the *italiano medio* within the socio-cultural context of the economic miracle, Sergio Rigoletto rightly interprets the *italiano medio* to embody a discursive process that delimits normality and ordinariness, and that creates 'this cinematic construct as an image of potential collective identification for the nation' (2007: 34). In other words, what is perceived as the 'national character' (Patriarca 2010: 266).

Berlusconi's self-inscription of his body within the category of Italian-ness has political consequences. In fact, it removes the stigma of the *italiano medio*, offering instead a genealogical masculine connection to a cultural and political context that precedes Berlusconi's historical persona and is linked to the notion of 'anti-politica' (anti-politics). In his discussion of *Berlusconismo*, Giovanni Orsina examines the origin and political constituency of the so-called *L'Uomo Qualunque* (the Everyman), an ephemeral political movement founded in postwar Italy by activist Guglielmo Giannini (chap. 2, Kindle ebook). Orsina maintains that the disappearance of that movement left a void that could be filled only by another movement or party inspired by a political outsider with which the bourgeois constituency could identify — that is, an 'everyman', or an *italiano medio*. According to Orsina's analysis, this space was temporarily and improperly filled for about four decades by the Christian Democrats, who maintained a strong consensus thanks to their allegiance with the Catholic Church. However, in 1992, the pool of magistrates of the so-called *Operazione Mani Pulite* (Clean Hands Operation) indicted on corruption charges the leadership of the Christian Democratic and Socialist parties, as well as some of the most powerful Milanese entrepreneurs. This wiped away the two major moderate parties (DC and PSI). *Mani Pulite* gave the Communist Party an unprecedented dominant position and left the political void of the *uomo qualunque* ready to be filled by Berlusconi. Orsina argues that Berlusconi answered the call of the 'civil society' for a leader who was remote from the left-wing parties and from the rhetoric of anti-fascism that had dominated the culture of the First Republic (Orsina, chap. 3).

The cultural constructs of *italiano medio* and *uomo qualunque* can be easily identified in the *commedia all'italiana*. Indeed, the *commedia all'italiana* itself has political implications. Patriarca points out that at its outset, this sub-genre served to redevelop the relevance of transformism and reassess certain psychological traits, such as sentimentalism and lack of patriotism, that were ostracized during Fascism. Additionally, it shaped a new taxonomy of Italian 'vices' that necessitated its own vocabulary, such as *familismo* (familism) and *mammismo* (being a mama's boy) (2010: 240-41). Moreover, while the pre-WWII discourse on Italian 'vices' and 'virtues' had contributed to ideas of transformation and hope from an anthropological and social perspective, in the *commedia all'italiana*, the depiction of the *italiano medio* articulated a cynical view of the national self (242-43). The types of the *italiano medio* became progressively more negative. Amongst others, the '*mammone*' (mama's boy), the '*vitellone*' (loafer), the 'politico opportunista o trasformista' (opportunistic or transformist politician), the cynical physician, the hypocritical moralist, and the tyrannical policeman are male protagonists in comedies featuring Alberto Sordi — the epitome of the *italiano medio* — such as: Federico Fellini's *I vitelloni* (The Big Loafers, 1953), Luigi Zampa's *L'arte di arrangiarsi* (The art of Figuring It Out, 1954), *Il vigile* (The Street Policeman, 1960), and *Il medico della mutua* (The Primary Care Physician, 1968), and Giorgio Bianchi's *Il moralista* (The Moralist, 1959), among many others (see Patriarca, 244-49).

The *italiano medio* presented by Sordi may be seen as a cynical response to the economic boom, as Stephen Gundle suggests (Baransky, Lumley 1990: 195-224), but it does not seem to present a social critique (Patriarca: 249). On the contrary, the evolution of the icon of the *italiano medio* to a vile, corrupt, arrogant, and tyrannical bully illustrates a process of adjustment to the economic and cultural changes brought by consumerism. This transformation contributes to a new understanding of Italian-ness as mediocre, dishonest, and exaggeratedly individualist, while conveying a political message of *qualunquismo* (political apathy).

La più bella serata della mia vita

We can look to Ettore Scola's 1972 comedy *La più bella serata della mia vita* (The Most Wonderful Evening of My Life) in order to expand on Berlusconi's symbolic self-presentation as the *italiano medio* and the concurrent stigmatization of Berlusconi as the bearer of moral degradation in Italian society. As we have seen, both this symbolism, which has political ramifications, and its open condemnation are profoundly engrained in the *commedia all'italiana*.

La più bella serata is a black comedy staging a mock trial of a corrupt and amoral proto-Berlusconi character, Alfredo Rossi (Alberto Sordi). Rossi is an Italian businessman who is driving to Switzerland to illegally transfer a hundred million lire. The story is drawn from the 1956 Swiss novel by Friedrich Dürrenmatt, *Die Panne* (the breakdown, US trans. *Traps* 1960) and the film is Scola's first adaptation of a work of fiction. As Stefano Masi points out, Sergio Amidei's script is much more pessimistic than *Die Panne* because it characterizes Alfredo as a cynical money-maker, who puts his Maserati above everything else, including friendship, love, loyalty, or any other values (2006: 45-46). The plot starts with with Alfredo who has attempted and failed — it is late and the bank is closed — to deposit money that he received in an under-the-table exchange. In a parking lot, he tries to strike a conversation with an attractive and enigmatic female motorist, whose face he cannot see because of her black helmet. She leaves without speaking and Alfredo, hoping for a hookup, chases her deep into the alpine countryside until his Maserati breaks down in the middle of the mountains. Seeking for help, he arrives at a sinister, isolated castle, where he meets four noblemen (Michel Simon, Charles Vanel, Claude Dauphine, and Pierre Brasseur) who entertain themselves by holding mock trials for historical characters and occasional guests. They invite him to stay and partake in his own trial. Alfredo, attracted to beautiful waitress Simonetta (Janet Agren), accepts the invitation hoping to satisfy his sex drive. The mock trial is carried out around a formal dinner, during which the four hosts question Alfredo on his life and work and debate their findings. In a 'climate of incumbent tragedy' (50), Alfredo's eloquent speeches progressively construct a strikingly amoral portrait of a man who has placed cheating and opportunism at the center of his personal and professional life. He candidly admits that his rise to power is the outcome of an affair with the wife of his former boss. He explains in detail how he orchestrated the man's death and inherited his patrimony, in cahoots with his lover. He then broke up with the woman and

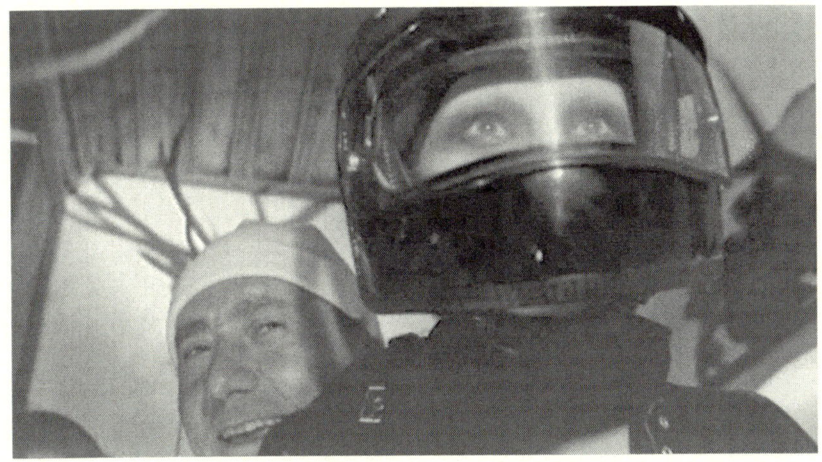

Figure 1. Simonetta riding Alfredo around the castle during Alfredo's
nightmare of his execution.

started laundering money and organizing call girl hookups for
his former boss's friends. In the closing arguments of the mock
trial, the 'prosecutor' portrays Alfredo as a shameless, corrupt,
and depraved criminal, and moves for the death penalty. The de-
fense of Alfredo's 'attorney', on the contrary, depicts an inept
man whose patrimony originated by chance and not personal talent, since he was neither able to succeed as a professional nor be
a proficient criminal.[3]

The entire film is based on this contradictory characterization
of Alfredo. A *nuovo ricco* (new wealthy man) of modern Italy's
consumerist society, Alfredo is in fact both a cynical egotist, who
only pursues his own interests, and an inept bumbler, who is ill-
equipped to achieve his goals. Blind to the awkwardness of the
situation, he is fascinated by the crude portrayal that his mock
'attorney general' gives of him. He is proud to be depicted as a
transgressive antihero and to be sentenced to death. *La più bella
serata* ends gloomily. After leaving the castle, Alfredo meets again
the anonymous female motorist who led him there in the first
place and he chases her one more time. This time the brakes

---

3   For an extended discussion on the figure of the 'inept' in Comedy Italian
     Style, see Jacqueline Reich (2004).

of his Maserati stop working and he falls into a ravine, thus self-executing the sentence of the mock trial. During the fall, he sees the female motorist finally taking off her helmet and revealing her identity as the castle waitress Simonetta.

The sexual power emanating from Simonetta, who plays the mythological role of the black angel of death, and Alfredo's comic debacle as a womanizer guide the death narrative. The night before his departure — and death — Alfredo has a nightmare where the not-yet-revealed Simonetta rides him on her motorcycle within the castle (figure 1) and eventually brings him to a grotesque medieval-style execution. But it is the final scene that turns the comedy into a dark tragedy that epitomizes the condemnation of Alfredo's type and the bourgeoisie that he represents. The fall through the air of the Maserati, in which Scola wanted to show Alfredo's becoming aware of his own misery (Masi: 46), is shot using a special camera for car crash-tests that produces an extreme slow motion effect (Ibid.) and shows the Maserati dramatically hanging in the sky (figure 2). The editing juxtaposes extreme low-angle close-ups of Simonetta contemplating Alfredo's death from a position of domination (figure 3) with extreme high-angle close-ups of Alfredo's face looking at her from the

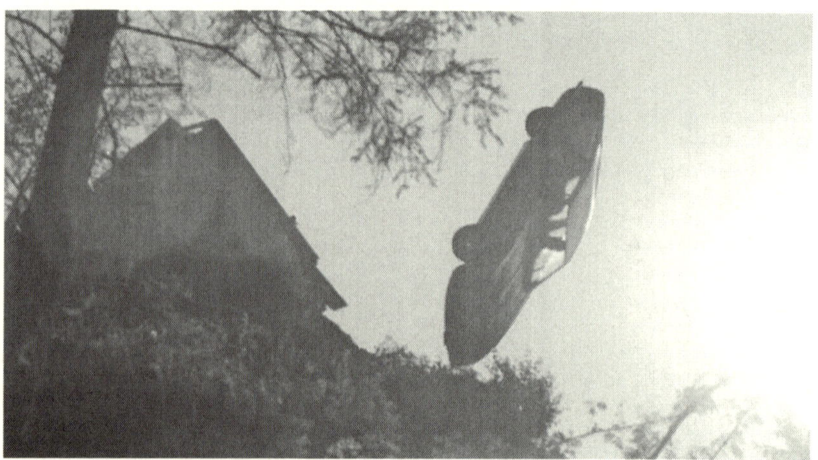

Figure 2. The long slow-motion shot of the Maserati precipitating
from the ravine.

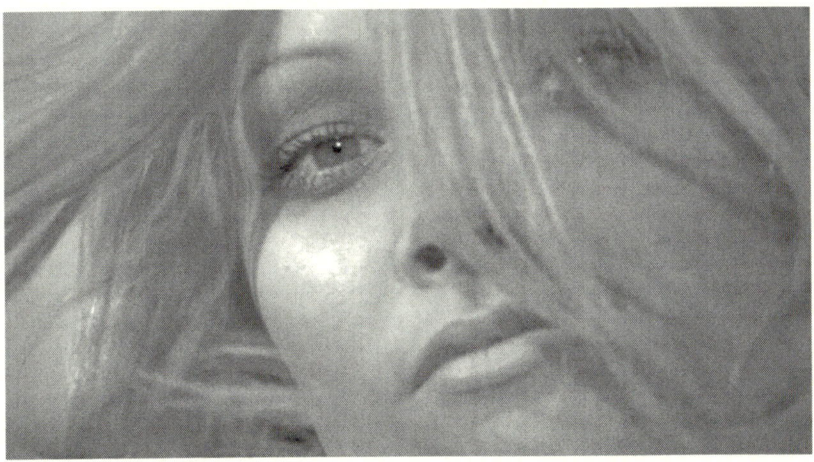

Figure 3. Extreme close-up, low-angle shot of Simonetta staring at Alfredo
in the death scene.

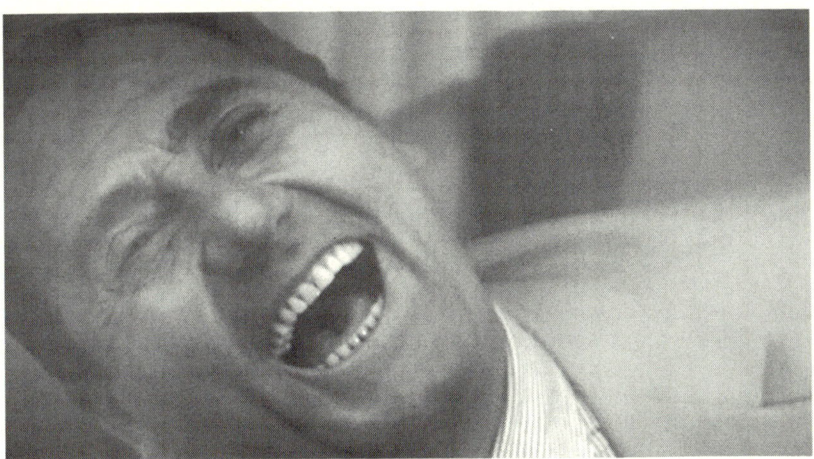

Figure 4. Extreme close-up, high-angle shot of Alfredo's laughter while
he is precipitating and apparently looking at Simonetta.

car compartment and expressing contrasting feelings, including caustic laughter (figure 4).

Alfredo foreshadows Berlusconi in a number of ways. First of all, there are social and biographical analogies between his background and Berlusconi's historical persona: Berlusconi, too, is a *nuovo ricco* (new wealthy man); his patrimony has an unclear origin; his relationship with justice and with the magistrates is problematic to say the least; he is outspoken about being a tombeur de femmes; and he is apparently obsessed by sex. The final execution orchestrated by a silent but dominating Simonetta also foreshadows Berlusconi's downfall, which, as Dominijanni suggests, also took place in the context of sexuality, when 'several female voices shouted "the king is naked"' and brought about his progressive elimination from parliament (2014a: 26). Even more significant than the biographical elements, however, is the symbolic mix of the stereotypical *italiano medio* traits that make Alfredo such a powerful proto-Berlusconi figure. Alfredo is the everyman, but also represents a constant oscillation between ineptitude and Machiavellian behavior and embodies an uncontrollable longing for sexual enjoyment.

This logic, I would argue, is at play in Berlusconi's public performance. Here the resemblance with Alfredo Rossi is truly striking. Back in 1995, for example, Berlusconi's official biography listed the main features of the *Cavaliere*'s personality and leadership. Some of these qualities are: 'stubbornness, volubility, unpredictability, unscrupulousness, ambiguity, self-reliant walk across the labyrinth of secrets [...], sense of clan, taste for command, propensity to control, attention for the attractive gesture, desire to please' (Fiori: 41). During the 2001 electoral campaign, Berlusconi's party *Forza Italia* (Go Italy) sent each Italian household *An Italian Story* (2001), a glossy 128-page biography of the leader, and a letter signed by Berlusconi himself. In the sections describing 'The Man' (4-41) and 'The Sports-fan' (60-67), Berlusconi is characterized by an 'irrepressible and outgoing vitality' (9), a 'cult for family' (13), a blind devotion to his mother (8-10, 19), an enthusiastic passion for soccer, and an ability to make money even in slightly dishonest — but socially acceptable — ways, such as doing homework for his classmates when he was in high school (10). The volume also emphasizes the envy of Berlusconi's young friends for his charm, fashionable look, intense social life, aura of success with girls, and talent for performance and singing (9). This can be seen as a subtle hint at Berlusconi's public performance of a vigorous sexual life, which would fully emerge several years later with the sex scandals, the *bunga bunga* parties, and allegations for underage prostitution.

In other words, since the beginning of his political career, a public narrative has been constructed to depict Berlusconi as a resourceful self-made man bearing the psychological traits, social behavior, and drives associated with the stereotypical idea of Italian-ness. These qualities also include the negative ones that are deemed positive by Italian society. In his discussion of Berlusconi's ascent to power within the national and international context, Perry Anderson elaborates on Berlusconi's main quality, 'spregiudicatezza', a word that does not have an equivalent English translation (2000). He emphasizes that this word connotes a mix of qualities that are usually perceived as conflicting. Indeed, 'for the Italians *spregiudicatezza* signifies, indivisibly, both admirable open-mindedness and deplorable ruthlessness. In theory, the context determines which [one] applies. In practice, common usage erodes the distinction between them' (Ibid.).

Spregiudicatezza in all matters of life and work is the main characteristic of both Adolfo Rossi and Silvio Berlusconi. Its conflicting meanings bring to the fore the tension between two dialectic forces, namely: the drama of the individual who struggles to adapt to social conventions while simultaneously recognizing the society's repulsion towards him (Grande 2003: 45). This conflict emphasizes, albeit in a hyperbolic fashion, the 'aberrant, abnormal everyday life, [that is] dominated by the most unbridled individualism and by a surplus of subjectivity that results in failure and defeat' (55). In other words, it is in the discursive construction of Italian-ness and *spregiudicatezza* of Comedy Italian Style that the proto-Berlusconi chronotype offers its best performance — and its model of moral degradation.

2.
SHIFTING BODIES:
ESTRANGED REPRESENTATIONS

We are ghosts that come from darkness and return into darkness.
Ginger e Fred

Auteur cinema has explored the semiosis of Berlusconi's body politic with a mix of repulsion and fascination. Federico Fellini's *Ginger e Fred* (Ginger and Fred, 1985) is the first feature film that openly deals with the influence of Fininvest-controlled networks on Italian society and cinema in the early 1980s. At the time of *Ginger e Fred*, Berlusconi had not yet entered the field of politics, and Fellini's criticism focused mainly on the practice of commercial interruptions during the broadcasts of feature films on Berlusconi's networks. His visionary sensitivity powerfully foreshadowed the cultural and philosophical implications that would become central in the oppositional discourses against Berlusconi. Yet there was a twenty-year period before the 'young' auteurs actually engaged in the representation of *Berlusconismo*. In this chapter, after a brief discussion of *Ginger e Fred* that I use freely as a bridge between past and present, I explore Nanni Moretti's *Il caimano* (The Caiman, 2006), Marco Bellocchio's *Bella addormentata* (Dormant Beauty, 2012), and Roberto Andò's *Viva la libertà* (Long Live Liberty, 2013). Of these films, only *Il caimano* centers on Berlusconi, but all three deconstruct the iconic and symbolic forms of Berlusconi's body politic in interesting ways. As a result, I discuss them as a united corpus.

Ginger e Fred *and the Sausages of* Cavaliere *Fulvio Lombardoni*

With *Ginger e Fred*, Federico Fellini brings to the fore his auteurist preoccupations about the integrity of film as a form of art. Fellini did not reject television as a medium per se; indeed, he admitted 'some fascination with the potential of television' and directed several advertisements, which helped him fund his last films (Ricciardi 2012: 51). However, he witnessed a time of profound transformation in Italian media. In 1984, the so-called 'decreto salva-private' (a decree to save the networks) prevented the shutdown of the networks controlled by Fininvest and allowed a rampant escalation of advertisement in television (Grasso 2000: 406). A wild deregulation ensued and only in 1990 did the 'legge Mammì' (Mammì law) establish clear rules concerning media monopoly, advertisement, live broadcasting, and film rating (514).

Fellini furiously rebelled against the interruption of films with ads, a new practice that Berlusconi's networks imposed on the Italian media market. His fight had legal ramifications: he brought lawsuits against Fininvest *Canale 5* (Channel 5) for inserting commercial breaks during the broadcasts of his films, *Lo sceicco bianco* (The White Sheik, 1952), *I vitelloni* (1953), *La dolce vita* (1960), and *8½* (1963). The legal controversy ended in favor of Berlusconi, legitimizing the standard of 'flow' that the spectatorship had already absorbed *de facto* (Minuz 2012: 219) within the framework of neotelevision (Williams 1974). However, Fellini's solo battle against the 'indiscriminate flooding' of commercials (Ricciardi: 54) in the name of the art of cinema consolidated his status as a '*uomo-simbolo*' (man-symbol) in the cultural panorama of postmodern Italy (Marcus 2002: 13). In fact, as Marcus emphasizes, Fellini's persona embodied 'that period when cinema occupied a position of cultural primacy — when films were seen as foundational acts, as socially defining exercises, as interventions in the life of the country. In short, Fellini stands for a time when filmmaking mattered' (Ibid.).

If in postmodern Italy, Fellini symbolizes the intellectual stature of the cinema 'that mattered', *Ginger e Fred* is the director's cinematic testament to the oppositional discourses about television. *Ginger e Fred* is the story of two elderly vaudevillian artists and tap dancers, Amelia Bonetti (Giulietta Masina) and Pippo Botticella (Marcello Mastroianni), who are invited to a television show titled *Ed ecco a voi* (We Are Proud to Present), more than twenty years after they ended their artistic careers. In the show, Amelia and Pippo have accepted to perform one of their famous tap dances in the style of 1930 American *divi* Ginger Rogers and Fred Astaire. In fact, the whole program of the show consists of caricatural performances in the televisual version of a Fellinian cinematic circus (Marcus: 184). This spectacle is juxtaposed with the romantic and nostalgic story of Amelia and Pippo, creating two conflicting narratives that Fellini ironically unifies by interspersing a number of fake commercials, posters, and other paraphernalia between the scenes. The commercials mainly advertise food and display gross erotic symbols, like hyper-sexualized and objectified female models eating phallic sausages. Opening and closing the film is the appalling predatory presence of an enormous *zampone* (pig's trotter), hanging from the ceiling of a train station in Rome (figure 5). The *zampone* can be understood as a visual metaphor of *Cavaliere* Fulvio Lombardoni — clearly alluding to *Cavaliere* Silvio Berlusconi — who is evoked throughout the film as a sort of venerated Big Brother, owning all the brands and

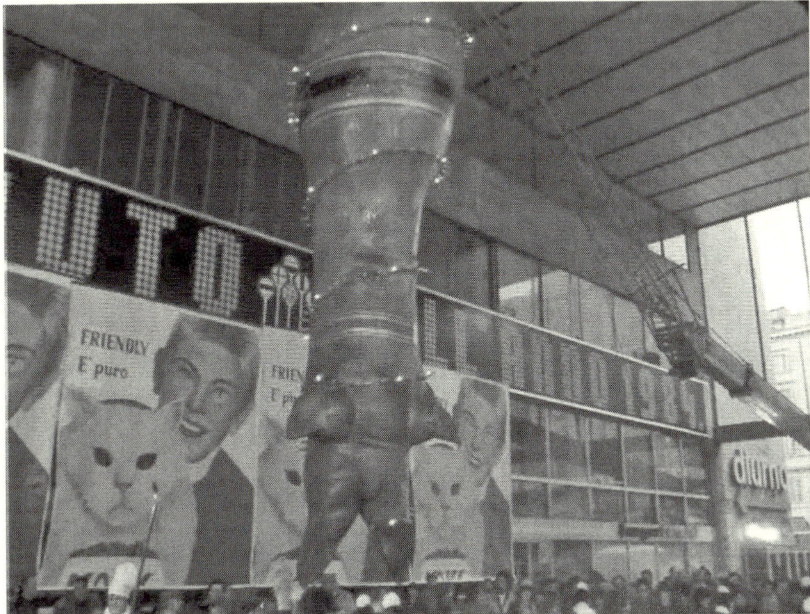

Figure 5. The *zampone* hanging from the ceiling of the train station in Rome in the opening sequence of *Ginger e Fred.*

even the television itself. By mocking the use of ads in the Fininvest networks, Fellini paradoxically sabotages his own cinematic language to show how television can ultimately eradicate any sense of authorship and create an indistinct 'flow' of signifiers that obliterates the difference between texts and contexts. With his visionary sensitivity, Fellini identifies an ongoing phenomenon and some of the aberrations that would later emerge from it.

Ginger e Fred — a film masquerading as a film within a television program — is an indictment of television as a medium that reduces everything 'to the same level of insignificance' and to 'mere simulations of reality' (Bondanella 2002: 158). Yet, what is Fellini's ultimate message? What is the director's place in the new mediatized world of *Berlusconismo?* Marcus (193), Ricciardi (64-65), and Minuz (210-22) answer this question focusing on Fellini's 'political' perspective on the matter. Marcus and Ricciardi underscore Pippo's speech regarding the socio-historical role of the tap dance as an original form of communication for the black slaves in the cotton plantations. For Marcus, Pippo's speech voices the director's 'longing for the referent' and creates the 'manifesto of an art that refers beyond itself to the real circumstances of the performers' lives' (193-94). Ricciardi argues that Pippo proposes the idea of an art practice that is simultaneously a 'political project' of resistance and liberation (65). Minuz examines several paratextual elements (interviews and journalistic articles) and concludes that *Ginger e Fred,* alongside with Fellini's last cinematic production, is a 'sincere admission of dismay' and a conservative standpoint in the face of a new production of media content and communication (222).

Both stances — that is, the aspiration to a referential and 'political' art and the sense of 'dismay' vis-à-vis the ongoing media changes — are, in fact, present in the film. I would also argue that throughout the film, a sense of paralysis consistently heightens, surfacing via the trope of the blackout. The blackouts are moments of 'stylistic repose' (Marcus: 195) from the baroque semiosis of television and they critically detach both the characters and the spectators from the narrative action in accordance with a Brechtian 'alienation effect' (Ricciardi: 66-67). However, they also emphasize a sense of impotence, especially the first section, when Pippo and Amelia are planning to escape. Yet as the

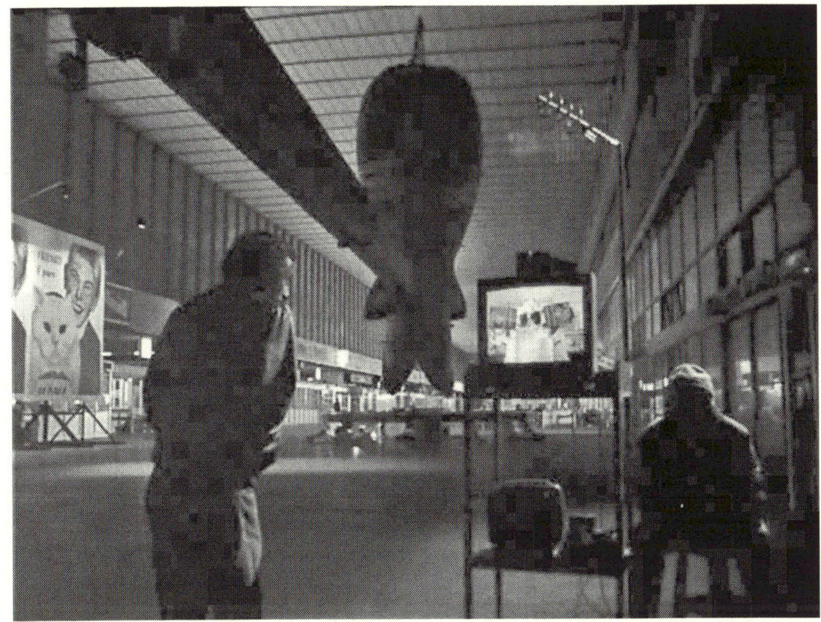

Figure 6. The final shot with the *zampone* hanging from the ceiling
of the train station

light comes back on, they are forced to stay and perform their tap dance for the public. The same sense of impotence emerges in the final shot of the *zampone* in the train station (figure 6). While the shot fades out into complete darkness, the sound gets louder, announcing *Cavaliere* Fulvio Lombardoni's entrance. This ending actualizes one of Pippo's aphorisms — 'we are ghosts that come from darkness and return into darkness' (*Ginger e Fred*) — which casts a gloomy shadow of self-defeat on the future. I would argue that the profound message of *Ginger e Fred* lies precisely in the paralyzing ambivalence between the longing for a referential, liberating art and this sense of impotence and self-defeat.

Deconstructing the Body Politic: Il caimano

'If only Nanni Moretti had the strength and clarity of purpose to make a film about Silvio Berlusconi. Instead, he has made a film about a film about Silvio Berlusconi' (Bradshaw 2006). Peter Bradshaw's review for *The Guardian* on Nanni Moretti's *Il caimano* (2006) is only one of the many unenthusiastic comments on the film. For a number of critics and progressive viewers, *Il caimano* did not fulfill their expectations because it was perceived more as a melodrama than a political film on Berlusconi (Dargis and Scott 2006). On the other hand of the spectrum, because of the film's coincidence with the 2006 political election, right-wing politicians affiliated with Berlusconi's party requested that the film's distribution be blocked. They feared that the circulation of a film on Berlusconi by a leftist director during the days of the election could affect the decisions of the electorate (Bonsaver 2007: 56). The film was not blocked, since it was broadcast from *Sky Cinema* in 2007. However, while the public television channel RAI 3 acquired the copyright for five years and maintained an intention of showing *Il caimano* at least five times, it never did. In fact, for the past several years, the visibility of the film has been greatly reduced. It was shown again from the private television channel *La7* only in October 2013, on the occasion of Berlusconi's removal from the Italian Parliament after a definitive sentence of four years of detention (then converted to community service) for tax fraud.

Il caimano tells the story of Bruno Bonomo (Silvio Orlando), a B-movie producer in the middle of both an economic and a personal crisis. His production house is going bankrupt after the director Franco (Giuliano Montaldo) quits the project of a historical movie on Christopher Columbus's homecoming. At the same time, Bruno's wife and former B-movie actress Paola (Margherita Buy) wants a divorce. In this discouraging scenario, Bruno meets a young director, Teresa (Jasmine Trinca), who gives him a screenplay on the figure of Italian former Prime Minister Silvio Berlusconi. Without great conviction and not fully aware of the political ramifications of this project, Bruno accepts to produce the film. He will struggle through economic and technical difficulties, retractions and refusals from the actors, the emotional and logistical consequences of separating from his wife, and depression. Despite all of this, he will continue to shoot through the final sequence, which closes the actual film. This is the notorious sequence of Silvio Berlusconi (Nanni Moretti), or the *Caimano*, who leaves the *Palazzo di Giustizia* (Palace of Justice) in Milan after the sentence to four years of prison, while a violent protest in his support starts in the *Palazzo*. This sequence has been called prophetic, because it foreshadowed not only the 2013 sentence for tax fraud, but also the protest by Berlusconi's supporters that took place in front of the same *Palazzo* in Spring 2013, after one of the *bunga bunga* trials. In that trial, Berlusconi was sentenced to seven years of detention for paying Karima El Mahroug aka 'Ruby Rubacuori' in exchange for sexual services when she was a minor. He was also facing charges for *concussione* (abusing his office), because he allegedly placed pressure on the head of the police to release Ruby Rubacuori from detention, stating that Ruby was related to former Egyptian President Hosni Mubarak.

La7 broadcasted *Il caimano* as a part of the talk show *Film Evento*, conducted by *La7* news broadcast director Enrico Mentana. The heated discussion of the *Film Evento* guests and the reaction of the media to the televisual event definitely promoted the political reassessment of a film that many had dismissed for 'lack of confrontational engagement with its subject' (Sutton 2000: 143). The debate highlighted the problematic relationship not only between justice and politics, which was the most cogent topic at the time of the show, but also between media and politics. In fact, the film powerfully stages the conflicting relationship between politics and media from both a narrative and figurative standpoint. In particular, it does so 'in terms of what is not seen of the actual film *Il caimano* within Moretti's film; the film that couldn't be made because of the media power of Berlusconi' (Ibid.). I would argue that the treatment of Berlusconi's body is the most 'political' feature of *Il caimano*, albeit in a symbolic way. This concept, which has recently been discussed by several scholars (Uva 2012, De Gaetano 2012, Zucconi 2013, O'Rawe 2014, Tagliani 2014), also connects *Il caimano* to Marco Bellocchio's *Bella addormentata* and Roberto Andò's *Viva la libertà*.

The caiman, an opportunistic predator (a type of crocodile) that stealthily hides and targets the most abundant prey, is 'impersonated' in the film through four different bodies: Berlusconi himself and three actors — that is, Elio De Capitani, Michele Placido, and Nanni Moretti.[1] The real Berlusconi appears in archival footage, showing moments and contexts from different phases of Berlusconi's political career. These include, among other clips, an extract from his talk during a European Parliament debate, in which he insults German politician Martin Schultz for being a 'kapo' and defends the beauty of Italian landscape (figure 7), and a televisual passage from a press conference in which he justifies the gifts he gave to some female guests at his parties.

Elio De Capitani, an actor who bears strong resemblance with the actual Berlusconi, impersonates the ghostly image that inhabits Bruno's mind when he reads the screenplay and thinks of the film (figure 8). De Capitani-Berlusconi is shown across time and in different scenarios, creating a subplot that delves into the historical and mediated figure of Berlusconi. He appears first as an opportunistic businessman who, after miraculously finding a large sum of money — literally falling from the ceiling — , corrupts politicians and the financial police so as to advance his business. Then, he is shown as a spectacular soccer team owner, an overbearing media tycoon, and a threatening, corrupt politician. Berlusconi-De Capitani also gives the notorious talk of the 'descent into the field' that marked the real Berlusconi's first step onto the political field and his unexpected electoral victory in 1994. Bruno seems not fully aware that this image impersonates Berlusconi.

Michele Placido, the third impersonation of Berlusconi, plays the self-reflexive role of famous actor Marco Pulici, who initially accepts the part but eventually resigns in fear of compromising his artistic career (figure 9). Pulici, portrayed as a sex addict, is driven by desire and physiological impulses, and is also very concerned with his own professional image. While declaring his political distance from Berlusconi and his intention to engage his professional figure in a political film, Pulici is simultaneously captivated by the man's personality and is willing to bring it to

---

1   With regard to the title, *Il caimano,* Silvia Carlorosi highlights that Moretti was inspired by an extract from jurist Franco Cordero's comparison between Berlusconi and Mussolini. Cordero argues that Berlusconi does not have 'magnetic fluid', but only 'smiles of a *caiman,* overabundant gestures, hilarious effects'. (Cordero 2002: 15, quoted in Carlorosi 2012: 88. Added emphasis).

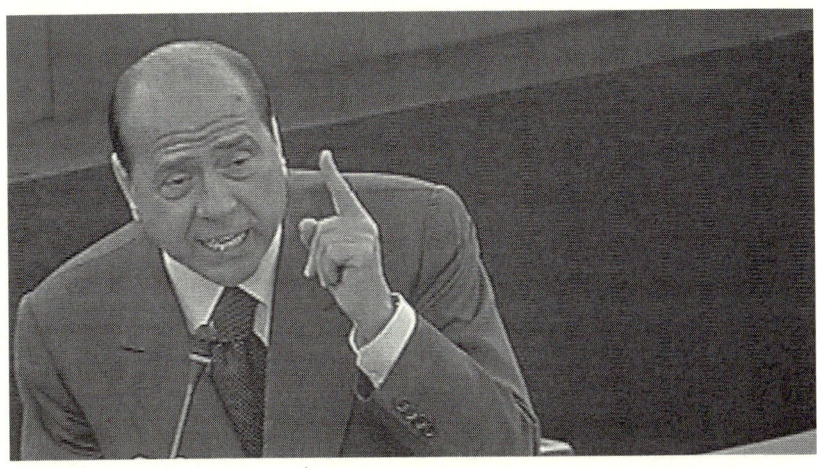

Figure 7. A still image from footage of Silvio Berlusconi during the 'kapo' attack in Strasburg.

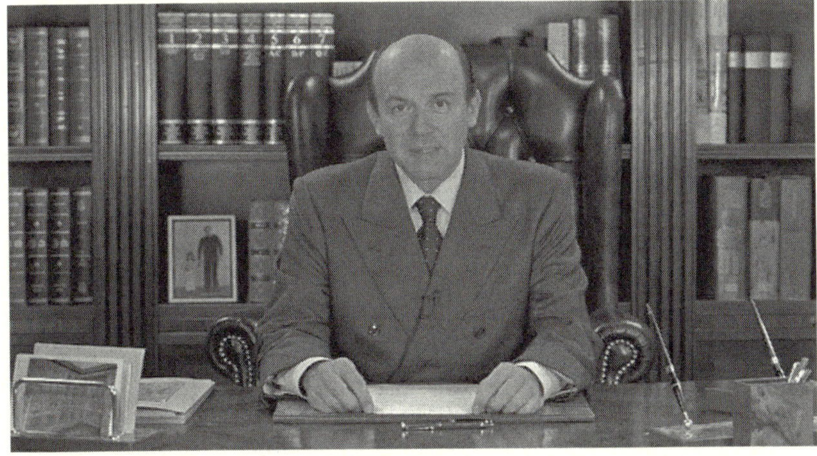

Figure 8. Elio De Capitani/Berlusconi during the speech of the *discesa in campo.*

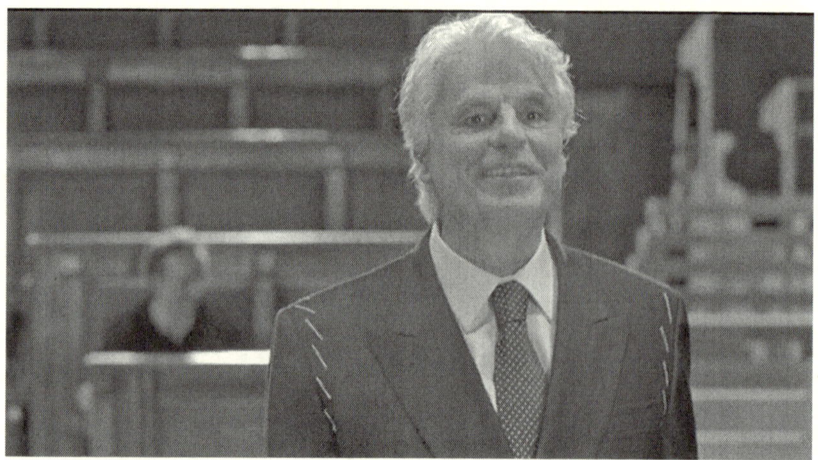

Figure 9. Michele Placido as a smiley Silvio Berlusconi during the rehearsals of *Il caimano.*

the stage. However, after shooting a few scenes in which he shows both his understanding of the man's performative skills — the seductive smile — and his fascination for him, he decides to not go ahead.

Nanni Moretti, (figure 10) who impersonates himself in the film, refuses to play the role of Berlusconi when Bruno approaches him. With the irony that characterizes his actorial persona, Moretti explains that he does not want to work in political dramas anymore but only in comedies. Eventually, Moretti lends his own body to the *caimano* that appears in the final and most dramatic sequence of the film within the film. Berlusconi/Moretti uses the words of the real Berlusconi to defend himself in the *Palazzo di Giustizia* and to call on his supporters to revolt in front of the *Palazzo.* Berlusconi/Moretti leaves in a taxi while the revolt is actually starting, and turns into a sinister shadow, finally revealed as the black caiman of the title that camouflages in the dark to attack its prey.

The fragmentation of Berlusconi's body into four representations and the discontinuity between the narrative film and the real Berlusconi (from the archival footage) demonstrate the director's strategic deconstruction of the complex semiosis of

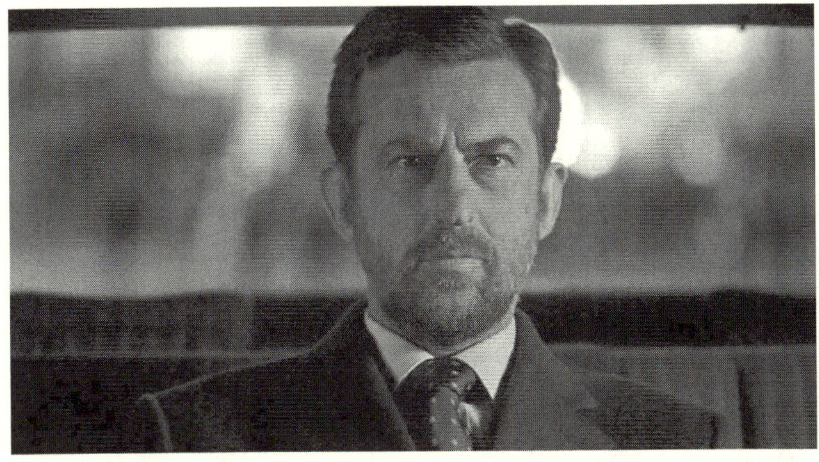

Figure 10. Nanni Moretti as the Caiman in the final sequence.

Berlusconi's body politic. Many scholars have emphasized the intrinsic difficulty of portraying Berlusconi in Moretti's film. Francesco Zucconi claims that the personification of Berlusconi's body through Bruno Bonomo's 'mental images' — that Bruno does not recognize as Berlusconi — points to the viewers' inability to understand Berlusconi's mediated reality (2013: 207-209). Clodagh Brook, too, emphasizes that 'visual medium is already saturated with his image' (2009: 120) and Catherine O'Rawe focuses on the complications of actorial impersonation and draws a connection to Berlusconi's fixation with his own body (2014: 160). Pierpaolo Antonello argues that Moretti is not interested in capturing the character's authenticity; instead, Moretti aims to create an 'impression of estrangement' (2012b: 51), one which produces 'parodic, grotesque, or even dramatic effects' (Ibid.). In this sense, the lack of mimetic realism provokes a detachment, or 'estrangement' — the so-called Brechtian effect of alienation — from the fictional narrative. This effect solicits the viewer's critical reception and promotes political awareness.

The multiple Berlusconis of Moretti's film clearly produce an effect of estrangement. The narrative plot is derailed by the dramaturgic effort to render Berlusconi's semiosis, and the four personas are seen through different performances of power — in the Foucaldian sense of 'techniques for "governing" individuals' (Foucault 1984: 337). In fact, each one of the four Berlusconis points to distinctive features of *Berlusconismo*:

1) Berlusconi/Berlusconi is the projection onto the public sphere of an uncomplicated individual reminiscent of the cynical characterization of the *italiano medio*;

2) Berlusconi/De Capitani impersonates the amplitude of the relationships between business, media, and politics;

3) Berlusconi/Pulici stages the erotic charge and seductiveness of the man's public performance;[2]

4) Berlusconi/Moretti signifies the instrumental use of political language to exert control on public discourses.

The four impersonations deconstruct the narrative on Berlusconi and generate a complex image, which hints at the pervasiveness and ubiquity of *Berlusconismo*. The film offers a metaphorical representation of this 'disassemblage' notion by staging Bruno's and his sons' obsession for Lego construction sets: after unsuccessfully seeking to build one, a myriad of Lego pieces eventually inundate Bruno's house, making it impossible to create a world that sticks together.

The finale of the film seems to not leave much hope: eventually the *caimano* has won, and both the action and the progressive darkness suggest a gloomy future for the country. However, the fact that the director eventually replaces the caiman's body with his own also calls into question the filmmaker's position within *Berlusconismo*. What are the implications of this substitution? Is Moretti's persona undergoing a monstrous metamorphosis or, on the contrary, is he unmasking the caiman and neutralizing the threat? In other words, is this finale an admission of self-defeat or an affirmation of agency? Roy Menarini argues that Moretti

---

2   Catherine O'Rawe points to Pulici intentionally taking on the challenge of engaging himself with the actorial style of Gian Maria Volontè, an Italian actor whose work was famously recognized as an act of political and civil engagement (2014: 158-59). This is in fact central to Pulici's characterization of Berlusconi and is his main motivation in accepting the job. However, Pulici eventually gives up the role, showing that he has fully absorbed the Foucaldian governmental techniques against which he wanted to stand as an actor.

performs an act of '*iconofagia*' (*iconophagy*) (2012: 108), that is, a sort of cannibalization of the caiman's image, using his own body to show the 'anthropological mutation' of contemporary Italy (109). Filippo Ceccarelli claims that the film is a 'big fight for the conquest of the imaginary' (2006), while Christian Uva emphasizes the 'descent into the field' of the director, who decides to use his own face to unmask the caiman (2012: 233). Francesco Zucconi points to Moretti's 'corpo *straniante*', which invites the spectator to rethink the whole plot and come to new awareness (210-11). These different interpretations depend on the fact that Moretti's film is a polysemic text, which may be seen as an example of 'strategic ambiguity', that is, an intentionally vague message by the text's creator (Ceccarelli 1998: 404-07).[3] As such, it can be understood in divergent ways, mainly with regard to the viewer's background or political perspective. It is also worth noticing that *Il caimano* and *Ginger e Fred* eventually devise the same question about the role of the filmmaker (self-defeat or agency?) in the time of Berlusconi.

Spectralizing the Body Politic: Bella addormentata *and* Viva la libertà

In Bellocchio's *Bella addormentata* (Dormant Beauty, 2012) and Andò's *Viva la libertà* (Long Live Liberty, 2013), Berlusconi does not have an obvious, central position. In fact, he appears infrequently in Bellocchio's film, and he never explicitly materializes in Andò's. However, in both films, Berlusconi is a spectralized body pointing to a political project. *Bella addormentata* and *Viva la libertà* capture certain symbolic dimensions of *Berlusconismo* that are pertinent to this analysis.

At the narrative crux of *Bella addormentata* is the theme of euthanasia and the case of Eluana Englaro, who was in a vegetative status for more than fifteen years. Her family asked for the possibility of assisted death, which triggered a widespread controversy in Italy. The film has four parallel narratives, all centering on euthanasia. First is the story of Rossa (Maya Sansa) a young female

---

3   See this book, pp. 12-13.

drug addict who has repeatedly attempted suicide, and Pallido (Piergiorgio Bellocchio), an ER physician who is determined to save her life. A second plotline focuses on the mother (Isabelle Huppert), father (Gianmarco Tognazzi), and brother (Brenno Placido) of a sixteen-year-old girl, left comatose after an accident. The mother has turned to faith and obsessively keeps vigils on her daughter in the hope of her reawakening. The most relevant thread for the discussion in this chapter is the story of Uliano Beffardi (Toni Servillo), a senator of Berlusconi's political coalition. During the days of the harsh debate on the Englaro case in the Senate, Beffardi is planning to vote against his party, which harshly opposes euthanasia. He has been personally affected by this issue because he secretly assisted his wife's death. After the event, his daughter Maria (Alba Rorwacher) has become a fanatic catholic and a supporter of the anti-euthanasia movement for the Englaro case. She engages in a romantic story (and this is the fourth plotline) with Roberto (Michele Riondino), but he sides with the pro-euthanasia movement and consequently, the relationship comes to an end.

A film on what Bellocchio defines the 'status of drowsiness' of contemporary Italy (Turrini 2012), *Bella addormentata* offers a particularly poignant representation of the political class, and of Berlusconi's coalition in particular. For example, the Senators of the *Popolo delle Libertà* (People of Liberties) are shown while bathing in a surreal spa. This image evokes a spatial and temporal

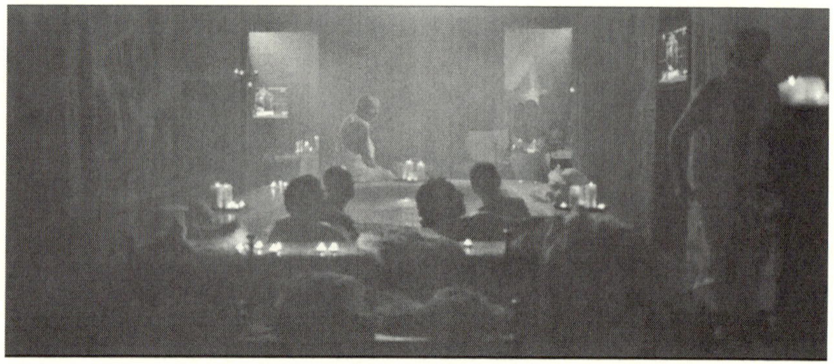

Figure 11. The senators bathing in the spa.

dimension blocked in ancient Rome, and is a powerful metaphor for the immobilism of Italian politics (figure 11). Immersed in thermal waters, the senators barely move — or do so slowly and clumsily — and are surrounded by a number of candles that give a sepulchral quality to the dark and foggy costume scene. The lack of referentiality, while increasing the symbolism of the scene, paradoxically creates a counter-narrative to the archival footage of politicians speaking about the Englaro case on television. The spa scene becomes the place for self-reflection, where Senator Beffardi — whose name in Italian means 'mocking' or 'sardonic' — converses with a psychologist (Roberto Herlitzka) on the political class and shares his anxiety about the legislation on euthanasia.

As symbolic as the spa scene is the photojournalistic service sequence. Ringing a long, empty table in a dark room, the politicians pose in front of the photographer, displaying an almost religiously inspired look as archival footage is projected behind them. The composition of the shot creates a frontal one-point perspective that converges on the projection, where a monumental Berlusconi appears during an official ceremony (fig. 12). While the images flow, the mise-en-scène and the montage of this complex sequence overlap the mediated images of the crowd celebrating Berlusconi with those of the politicians. Simultaneously, the bodies of the politicians are inundated by the overflowing col-

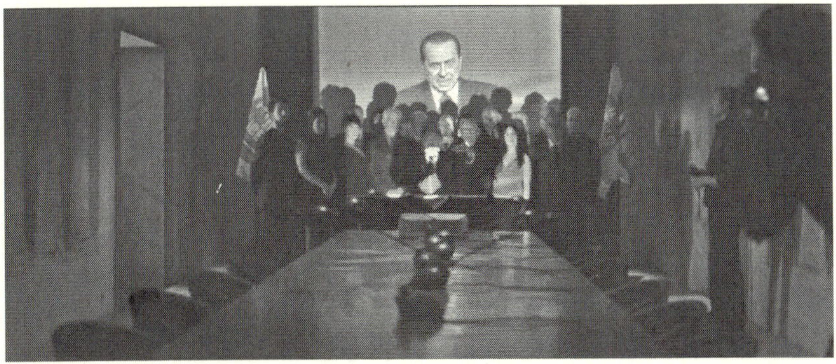

Figure 12. The politicians pose for the photographer, with Silvio Berlusconi projected on a screen behind and over them.

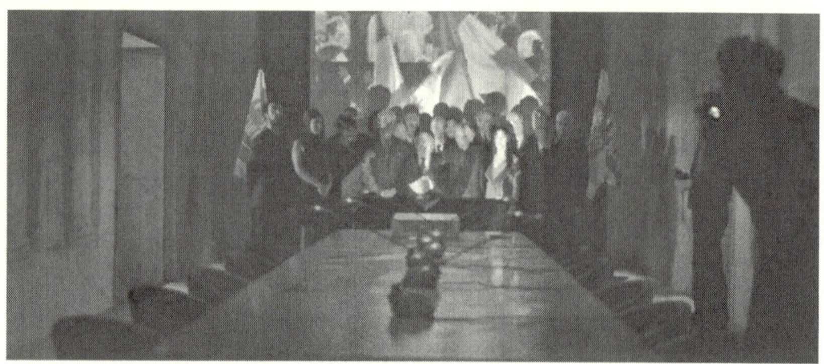

Figure 13. The politicians posing with Italian flags on the screen behind —
and again — over them.

ors, movements, and music of the footage (fig. 13). Because of its
central position, light, monumentality, and non-diegetic celebra-
tive sound, Berlusconi's footage is stripped of its documentary
function. Instead, the intermediality of the sequence suggests a
sort of political 'liturgy' in which the leader's body is virtually glo-
rified by 'acclamation' (Agamben: 256) both in its original context and in the fictional narrative. As Giacomo Tagliani (2014)
and Francesco Zucconi (2013) argue for Moretti's *Il caimano* and
Bellocchio's *Vincere* (Win, 2009), these films 'textualize the transformation of the character in its own image' (Tagliani: 208). In
Bella addormentata, Berlusconi's body is iconized from the beginning, there is no dramaturgic attempt to represent it. Here, Bellocchio is interested in the spectralization of the leader's body,
which stems from the 'multiplication, and dissemination of the
function of glory' (Agamben: 256) that emanates from the media
process of the 'society of the spectacle' (Debord 1967).

In Roberto Andò's *Viva la libertà*, Berlusconi's body is not even
an iconic presence, but is symbolically alluded to through other
bodies and signifiers of his own self. The seductiveness of the
body is, in fact, the central theme of the film and bears certain
political implications that deserve attention.

An entertaining political apologue, *Viva la libertà* is adapted
from the director's own novel, *Il trono vuoto* (The Empty Throne,
2012). It stages the classic comic trope of the double in an origi-

nal and interesting way through the body of Tony Servillo, an actor who is 'celebrated for his versatility and ability to create different characters' (O'Rawe 2014: 154).[4] Servillo in this film performs two roles: that of the secretary of the Democratic Party, Enrico Olivieri; and that of his twin brother, Giovanni Ernani, a former academic who has a psychological disorder and has been living in a mental institution for many years. In the middle of the national electoral campaign, Olivieri is losing substantial support and is on the verge of depression. After another drop in the polls and an increasing number of protests against him, he decides to take a break and flee to Paris to his friend Danielle (Valeria Bruni Tedeschi). Nobody knows of Olivieri's absence, except his assistant, Andrea Bottini (Valerio Mastrandrea) and his wife (Michela Cescon). Out of desperation, the two decide to temporarily replace Olivieri with Ernani. It is a big risk because of Ernani's mental disorder. Unexpectedly, Olivieri/Ernani's utopian vision and passionate speeches soon create a spark in the electorate and bring him great popularity. During Olivieri/Ernani's performance as a politician, Olivieri is in France, enjoying himself on set, and helping out his friend, who is a film editor and the wife of a film director. Election Day comes and the Democratic Party wins easily, but Olivieri/Ernani suddenly disappears, while Olivieri leaves France. In the final scene, Bottini (the assistant) comes face to face with an enigmatic double character that seems to typify the personalities of both twins. Is he Olivieri or Olivieri/Ernani? The character looks at Bottini, then into the camera, shifting from the serious confidence of Olivieri to the seductive smile of Olivieri/Ernani. The question is left unanswered (figures 14 and 15).

I would argue that the trope of the double in *Viva la libertà* not only spectralizes Berlusconi's semiosis, but it also incorporates the main traits of his public self through the body of a conflicting leader. The seductive smile is one of these traits and it is shown unambiguously as a positive quality throughout the film. After all, it is thanks

---

4   Servillo's performances of politicians include Giuseppe Mazzini in Mario Martone's *Noi credevamo* (We Believed, 2010), Giulio Andreotti in Paolo Sorrentino's *Il divo* (2009), and Uliano Beffardi in Bellocchio's *Bella addormentata*, that is briefly presented in this chapter.

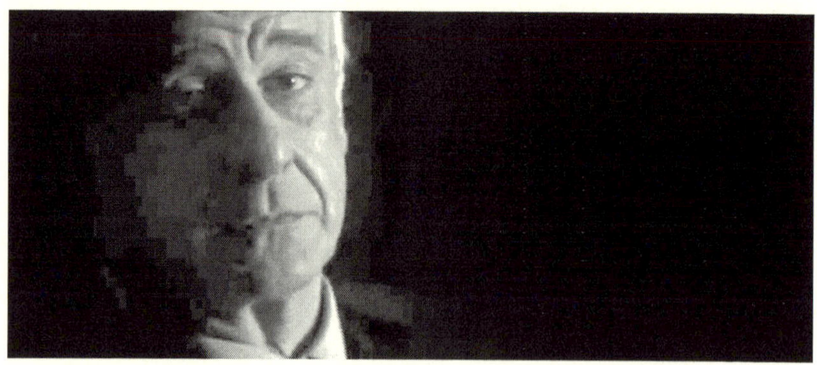

Figure 14. Olivieri (or Olivieri/Ernani) looks grimly at Bottini.

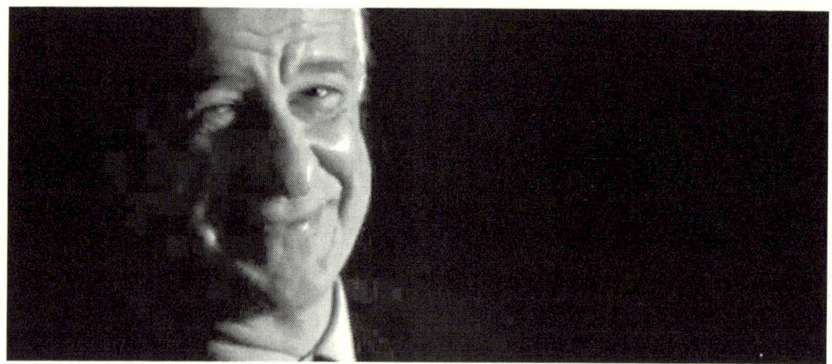

Figure 15. Olivieri (or Olivieri/Ernani) smiles at Bottini.

to Olivieri/Ernani's empathy and sentimental call on the electorate that the Democratic Party wins the elections in the film. In this sense, the character's final gaze into the camera seems to perform an act of 'interpellation' (Casetti 1998: 16-18) that questions the viewer's understanding of the political message of the film.

This challenge is brought about in the film quite explicitly through the conflicting bodies of the twin brothers. In fact, Olivieri/Ernani allows bodily expression, emotions, and sexual drives to enter the political sphere and offers a performance of self (Goffman 1959) that is joyous and seductive. For example, as in Berlusconi's notorious electoral campaign in 2001, Olivieri/Ernani presents himself as the friendly candidate in a variety of contexts — in schools, in construction sites, in hospitals. There are also moments when he demonstrates a certain degree of transgression. As Minuz (2013) points out, one of these moments is Olivieri/Ernani's visit to the German Chancellor — clearly evocative of Angela Merkel — with whom he engages in a passionate barefoot tango. Spying from the peephole, Bottini is astonished (figure 16). Later in the film, Bottini and Olivieri/Ernani clarify Bottini's bewilderment for his positive feelings toward the candidate. Here is the dialogue:

> BOTTINI   I'd like to confess you something. I'm shivering just for thinking of it. [pause] I'd vote for one like you.
> OLIVIERI/ERNANI   And you feel guilty for this. Don't worry. It happens. It happens when one is scared of winning (*Viva la libertà*).

The conversation ends with a passionate hug between the two. Bottini's guilt is a reaction to Olivieri/Ernani's qualities that garner him support, but at the same time show his proximity to the hedonistic body politic of *Berlusconismo* — that is, *jouissance*, empathy, seduction, and even a touch of *spregiudicatezza*.[5] Additionally, Olivieri/Ernani's body is malleable and touchable: he can dance both with the German pseudo-Merkel and the guests of the

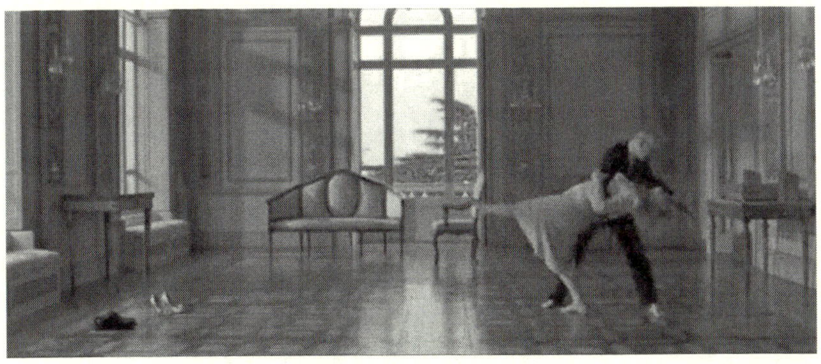

Figure 16. Olivieri/Ernani dances with the German Chancellor.

---

5   For a discussion of *spregiudicatezza* see this book, p. 39.

mental institute where he lives; he embraces people, including Bottini and his twin brother's wife; he smiles and eats with appetite; he kisses and is kissed. Olivieri is quite obviously his brother's specular image. He embodies an almost innate repulsion for emotions and sexuality. He is presented as rigid and untouchable. He barely smiles and is incapable of giving or receiving pleasure, as shown during the scene in the swimming pool with the semi-naked girl. His love for film is the only passion that revitalizes him during his stay in France. Yet, the idea of cinema that emerges from the conversations of Olivieri and his friends is mainly a nostalgic one. For example, Olivieri compliments Danielle because, as a film editor, she has the privilege to 'protect the order of the events from approximation, from nonsense' (Ibid.). It is with the same 'protective' logic, I would argue, that Danielle's husband (the film director) shows footage from Fellini's protest against the practice of commercial interruptions during the broadcasts of feature films on Berlusconi's networks in the 1980s (figure 17). It is quite interesting that with this final consideration, we are back where this chapter began.

In the films discussed in this section, Berlusconi's body appears in a variety of ways. In Fellini's *Ginger e Fred*, his presence is evoked by the fictional name of *Cavaliere* Fulvio Lombardoni and is implicated in the visual predatory metaphor of the *zampone*. In Moretti's *Il caimano*, Berlusconi's persona is deconstructed through a series of dramaturgic representations until its final replacement

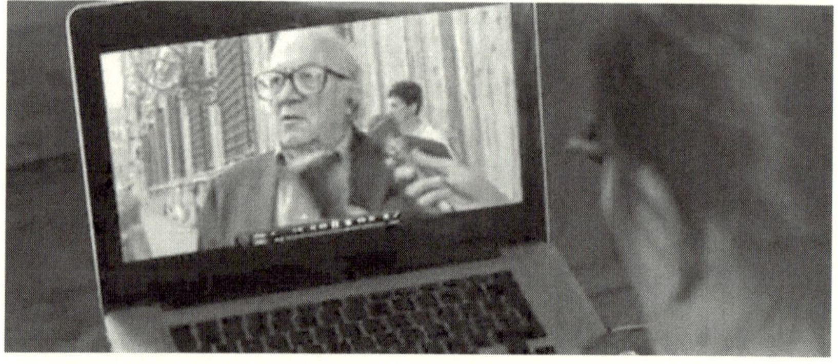

Figure 17. Danielle's husband watching a clip of Federico Fellini's protest against the commercial breaks in the Fininvest network.

with the director's own body. In Bellocchio's *Bella addormentata*, the leader's body is reduced to an icon and spectralized as the pure emanation and acclamation of political power. The ambiguous finale of *Viva la libertà* seems to affirm that the only possible way to solve the conflict between the two bodies — the low and the high, the bodily and the intellectual — consists of keeping alive and 'protecting' the old body while appropriating the seductive smile and the regime of enjoyment of Berlusconi's body.[6]

---

6   For a comprehensive discussion of the regime of enjoyment in *Berlusconismo*, see Domijanni (2014a and 2014b).

3.
BERLUSCONI *IN MORTE*:
KILLING THE KING'S BODY

Political assassinations are always shocking events. As Ron Eyerman suggests, 'the murder [...] of a public figure arouses feelings of identification, empathy, and loss among groups of people, even if they are not part of any political constituency in the narrow sense' (2011: xiv). For these reasons, assassination is a common theme in cinema, and has been codified in precise genres and sub-genres that elaborate on broad political contexts, such as the conspiracy thriller and the president-assassination plots. These films respond to the anxieties circulating in the social body after the assassination, helping to overcome the trauma. On the contrary, films on the imagined assassination of *living* political leaders are particularly controversial because they may set in motion processes of moral panic and actual threats. For example, the recent North American film *The Interview* (2014) had serious problems of theatrical distribution because of terroristic threats.[1]

This chapter discusses three feature films, which were recently produced in Italy on the imagined assassination of Silvio Berlusconi: *Bye Bye Berlusconi* (2005), directed by Jan Henrik Stahilberg, *Shooting Silvio* (2007), directed by Berardo Carboni, and *Ops... Ho ammazzato Berlusconi* (Oops... I Killed Berlusconi, 2008), di-

---

1   In the post- 9/11 era, interest in the theme of political assassination has increased. Recently, several films on the murder of living political leaders were produced, arising great controversies on the national and global scenes: the puppet-animated satire *Team America: World Police* (2004), directed by Trey Parker, which stages the impalement of former North Korean leader Kim Jong-il; the mockumentary *Death of a President* (2007), directed by Gabriel Range, which comments on the fictionalized assassination of President George W. Bush; and the political comedy *The Interview* (2014), directed by Seth Rogen and Evan Goldberg, that imagines the death of Korean dictator Kim Jong-un.

rected by Gianluca Rossi and Daniele Giometto. They were independent low-budget films and it goes without saying that all had problems of funding and distribution. *Bye Bye Berlusconi* is a German production with Italian actors and actresses who decided to work for free for political reasons. It received attention due to its inclusion in the Berlin International Film Festival in 2006, the year of *Il Caimano*, but eventually distribution in Italy was effectively blocked in a miasma of bureaucratic excuses and convenient confusion.[2] Only a very few copies of *Ops... Ho ammazzato Berlusconi!* were released. *Shooting Silvio* was released in Italy and France. *Cinedance* promoted it by throwing local parties where participants received tickets for the film. In 2009, *Shooting Silvio* was broadcast on *Sky Cinema*, the satellite network owned by Berlusconi's historical media enemy Rupert Murdoch. The film raised strongly negative reactions among Berlusconi's entourage and eventually its broadcasting was interrupted. Beatrice Lorenzin, a congresswoman and former member of Berlusconi's party *Popolo delle Libertà* or PDL, charged that it was 'a celebration of violence and an incitement to brutal actions against the man and against the Prime Minister Silvio Berlusconi' (*La Repubblica* 2009).[3] Nunzia De Girolamo, another former PDL member and congresswoman, called *Shooting Silvio* 'morally harmful' and accused the media of preparing an offensive storm against Berlusconi (Ibid.).[4] All three films are now available in DVD, although *Bye Bye Berlusconi* can only be bought through German retailers or streamed on YouTube.

---

2   There are long discussions on the Internet about the delays and rejections that eventually prevented *Bye Bye* from being distributed in Italy. The most reliable source seems a forum with posts from tonynx, who speaks of the film as 'ours' and explains all the passages in great details (2008).

3   Beatrice Lorenzin left Berlusconi's party in 2013 and is now affiliated with *Nuovo Centro Destra* (New Center Right), or NCD. She was Ministry of Health in the government led by Prime Minister Enrico Letta (Democratic Party, or PD) in 2013 and was confirmed by Matteo Renzi in 2014 (PD).

4   Nunzia Di Girolamo, too, left Berlusconi to join NCD in 2013 and was Ministry of Agricolture in Letta's government.

Mocking the Primal Scene: Bye Bye Berlusconi

One of the protagonists of *Bye Bye Berlusconi,* Lucia (Lucia Chiarla), in the film says, 'the best thing in Italy is that almost everyone is against the Prime Minister. When you want to make a film against him, all are enthusiastic. And when the moment to make it comes, someone has always a second thought.' But what does making a film against the Prime Minister by staging his assassination exactly mean? Which kind of political project does this film entail? I want to start the discussion with *Bye Bye* not only because it was made before the other two, but also because it stages a terrorist attack on Berlusconi — albeit in a grotesque and parodic mode — which seems reminiscent of the *anni di piombo* (years of lead) and the kidnapping and assassination of former Prime Minister and president of the Christian Democrats, Aldo Moro, at the hands of the Red Brigades, a left-wing radical group, in 1978.

Eyerman calls the assassination of John Fitzgerald Kennedy 'primal scene' because the event was broadcast live and 'visualized the collective reaction' of the nation (2). I would say that Italy's 'primal scene' is the 1978 kidnapping, sequestration and murder of Moro. The mediatizaiton of this dramatic event, which lasted fifty-five days, turned this event into an experience of collective trauma. The Moro case also gave birth to a cinematic trend, and overall it has become a common reference in Italian cinema. Alan O'Leary argues that the Moro kidnapping has 'become the key topic to be interrogated for any film with pretensions to political commentary' (2010: 152). *Bye Bye* is a political satire — with absurdist farcical elements — staging an attack on Berlusconi in the style of the 1978 Moro kidnapping. Several Moro-esque patterns are immediately recognizable to the viewers who are familiar with the trend, such as: the kidnapping and sequestration, the massacre of the escort guards — with bloody details on the bodies and car seats — the line of 'fermezza' (firmness) taken by the local authorities who refuse to negotiate, and the trial of the hostage from the hideout. A scene with the kidnappers at the kitchen table cutting up vegetables even suggests a comic parallelism with a scene from Marco Bellocchio's *Buongiorno, notte* (Good Morning, Night, 2003), where the terrorists prepare green beans for a vegetable soup (fig 18). In fact, *Bye Bye* establishes its parodic

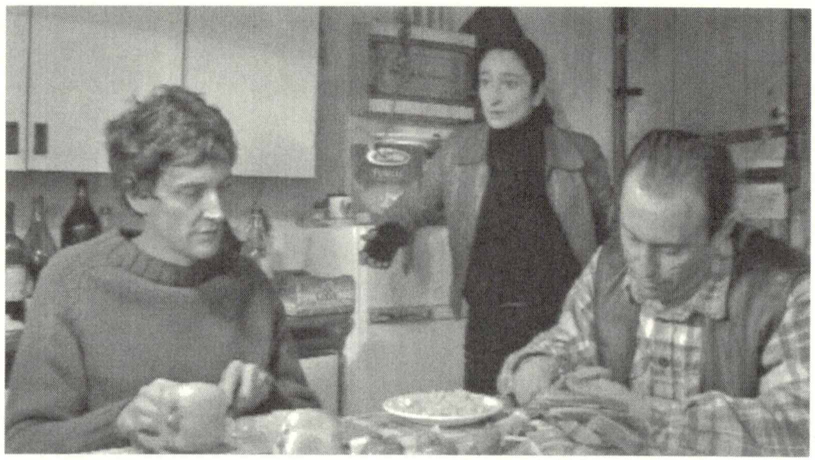

Figure 18. The three kidnappers in the hideout preparing a vegetable soup.

relationship with the Moro scene at the beginning of the film, by staging the sequence of the kidnapping on the sunny Riviera with cheerful non-diegetic music and the action of a slapstick comedy (when she closes the car's door, Lucia pretends she has broken a finger).

Self-reflexivity is in fact a central element — perhaps the most interesting one — in *Bye Bye,* which unfolds as a film within the film: the first layer is the video-diary documenting the difficulties of making a film on the sequestration of Berlusconi; the second layer stages the kidnapping, where other Moro-esque details also surface. The comic and dramatic modes intersect with the thriller in both levels, and the Moro pattern unifies the structure giving the film a light aura of *impegno* — albeit always on the edge of farce. The idea of political engagement is reinforced through the film by the sense of collective participation of the people of Montaretto di Bonassola, a small village on the Riviera Ligure where some of the external scenes were shot.

Bye Bye starts with Lucia's video-diary which provides a film chronology and documents censorship problems. The film begins with a sequence of the kidnapping, but filming is soon interrupted by the production lawyer (Fabio Bezzi). The filming is halted because the lawyer says the name of Berlusconi cannot be used without his permission. To get around this legal hurdle, the producer (Franco Leo) decides to use fictional names and change the whole project, switching from a political drama to a satirical fable — not without skepticism on the actors' part. The producer and director rewrite the names of the characters and locations' giving them pseudo-Disneyan nicknames: Berlusconi (Maurizio Antonini) becomes 'Topolino' (Mickey Mouse), mayor of 'Topolonia' and owner of the television channel 'Tele Anguria' (Water Melon TV).

The kidnappers (Pietro Ragusa, Tullio Sorrentino, and Pietro Bontempo) are renamed 'Banda Cazzotti' (Fists Band). The kidnapping can now be staged and the Banda takes the hostage to the hideout. The sequestration's plot is often interrupted by hypersexualized shows and commercial breaks on Tele Anguria, clearly evoking the Fininvest networks (figure 19). The trial begins from the hideout and the Banda Cazzotti accuses Berlusconi/Topolino of many of the offenses that Berlusconi has actually faced. The Banda also organizes a web video streaming of the trial and polls the viewers on each charge (figure 20). Viewer participation in the polling is very high and the Banda hopes to stage a collective 'last day of the King' (*Bye Bye Berlusconi*). Yet, the final sentence is not one of death. Since the polls have overwhelmingly condemned Topolino, the Banda decides to free him, believing that

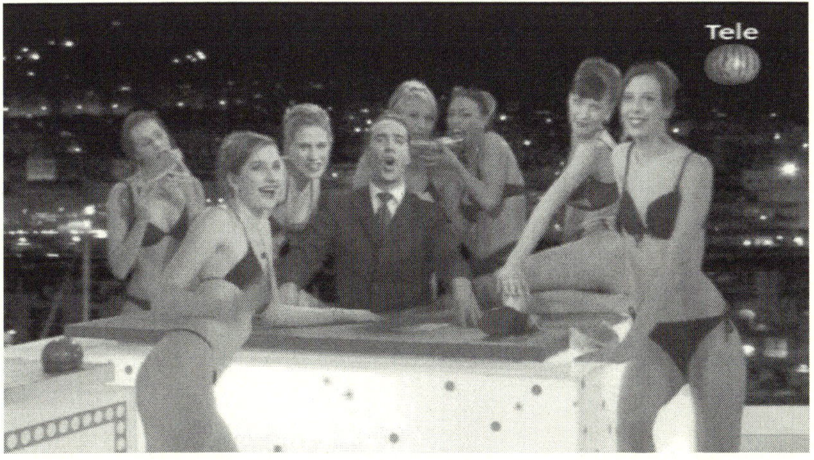

Figure 19. A moment of a show at Tele Anguria.

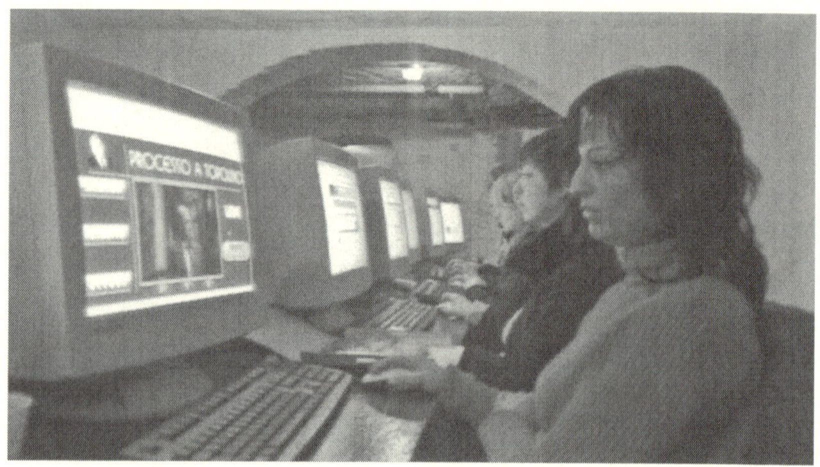

Figure 20. Internet poll on the trial of Topolino.

people themselves will eliminate him and his 'empire' (*Bye Bye Berlusconi*). This absurdist plot is complicated by the parallel story of the making of the film. In fact, the video-diary soon becomes a small thriller documenting a climax of events that threaten the lives of the Banda and their families. In the end, the documentary diary and fiction overlap: when Berlusconi/Topolino goes back to normal life Lucia and her friends are mysteriously killed.

An Apocalyptic Coming-of-Age: Shooting Silvio

Shooting Silvio is the first feature film by Italian director Berardo Carboni. It centers on the life of Gianni Crea, aka Kurtz (Federico Rosati), a nickname inspired by the Kurtz of Coppola's *Apocalypse Now.*[5] Kurtz, a wealthy young man living alone in a luxurious apartment in Rome after the death of his parents, feels deeply disgusted by contemporary society and the apathy of his generation. His disgust takes the form of an existential crisis into

---

5   Gianni (Giovanni) Crea is the name of a living Italian director of popular, or B-movies.

which he tries to drag his quirky friends, his girlfriend Sofia (Sofia Vigliar), and even his immigrant waiter (Alessandro Haber).

Kurtz is a writer, but is unhappy in his work and during a party he burns all the copies of his book. He models his own self on the characters of *Apocalypse Now* (1979) and Coppola's *Rumble Fish* (1983), living a vicarious experience through cinema. For example, he wears masks and spends his time alone contemplating his red fish — the only element in color within the black and white of the film (like the fish in *Rumble Fish*). Kurtz's eccentricity and provocative attitude also recalls the angry men of British cinema of the 1960s, such as Karel Reisz's *Morgan: A Suitable Case for Treatment* (1966). These cinematic references complicate Kurtz's rebellious attitude and solitary mind. After watching the American documentary *Citizen Berlusconi* (2003) and other footage, including the notorious 'kapo' rant against Mr. Schultz in the European Parliament, he begins to be obsessed by Berlusconi. He also starts dreaming of him. He has an interview with journalist Marco Travaglio, where he learns more about Berlusconi, and feels more and more claustrophobic and alone. It is after seeing Charlie Chaplin's final monologue from *The Great Dictator* that Kurtz decides to take action and actually kill Berlusconi. To this end, he seeks his girlfriend's and his closest friend's help, but they refuse and try to dissuade him. He finally finds a partner in his new love interest, the young black woman Melanie (Melanie Gerren). The plan is simple: she will distract Berlusconi and his escort guards by stripping in front of them during a public event. This distraction will allow Kurtz to break through the security system, kidnap Berlusconi, and finally kill him. The plan, which the film presents in the form of an animation, is successful: during Melanie's strip Kurtz is able to sequester Berlusconi, force him to wear a Marlon Brando mask, and run away with the Prime Minister in his BMW — the mask being a final allusion to *Apocalypse Now* (fig 21). In a long and trivial dialogue, Berlusconi begs Kurtz not to shoot him, but as the final credits start to roll a gunshot is heard.

The film is shot almost entirely in black and white, except for a few sequences during the film and the ending. This technique creates a sense of flatness that blends people, images, and the urban landscape together, and is used symbolically to mirror Kurtz's and his friends' feelings. The black and white should also give the viewer a sense of estranged space and time.

There are peculiar moments in this film. The big party that Kurtz gives at his place is one of them. During the party, Kurtz gives a magniloquent, theatrical speech to his guests — reminiscent of Kurtz's speech in *Apocalypse* —, in which he expresses the reasons for his *mal de vivre* and calls his guests to action, proposing a common objective. He explains that he wants to collectively write a book that discusses 'one hundred ways and one hundred reasons' to eliminate Silvio Berlusconi 'in all senses: physical, political, metaphysical, as anybody wishes' (*Shooting Silvio*) The monologue is worth reading, as it offers Kurtz's perspective:

> KURTZ   I feel sick. And you, too, I believe, are sick, but you don't even realize it. Every morning I wake up, I get up, I look around, and I see nothing but replicants, creatures that don't feel the air, fish… I unwillingly precipitated into a place that doesn't

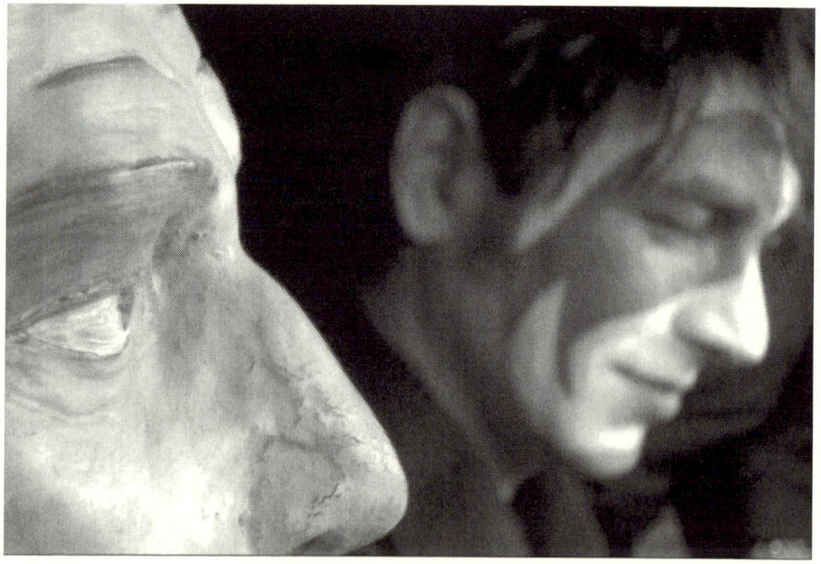

Figure 21. Kurz (on the right) before shooting Berlusconi, who is wearing the Brando mask.

belong to me, into a situation that is not mine. We have to try to come out from it, we have to get closer, recognize each other, get out from this damned individualism. I believe I identified the main cause of this collective failure, of this lack of logic, feelings, or memory. For months I've been groping in the dark. I couldn't see my future, our future anymore, it just wasn't there. Then, one day, the vision arrived. I visualized the tip of the iceberg, the spring of the river of aridity in which we all are drowning.

(Kurtz shows a giant picture of Silvio Berlusconi, upside down)

Do you recognize him? Yes, he's upside down, but the double-breasted jacket is the same, the smile is the usual one, unmistakable. He's Silvio Berlusconi, folks, our premier, the unquestioned symbol of this age without virtue.

I gathered you guys here tonight to find a way to react to this condition. I decided to write a collective book to try to demonstrate that there still are people who are able to say no. The idea is simple: each one of you will write a page. In each page you must list a way in which and a reason why to neutralize Berlusconi. Eventually, we'll have one hundred ways and one hundred reasons to eliminate him.

YOUNG WOMAN   *(from the public of Kurtz's guests)* But eliminating him … what do you mean exactly?

KURTZ   In all meanings. Physical, political, metaphysical, as anybody wishes. I have even the title: *Shooting Silvio.* (*Shooting Silvio.* Added emphasis)

Kurtz's monologue proposes the neutralization of Silvio Berlusconi as a collective solution for his and his generation's problems. Kurtz believes that his generation's individualism and lack of future can be cured by fighting together for shared values, such as humanity, reciprocity, memory, and rationality. The motivations and goal of this 'revolutionary' collective project converge naturally on the killing of Silvio Berlusconi. While Kurtz speaks, he shows a giant poster highlighting the iconic traits that make Berlusconi's body 'unmistakable', namely: the 'double-breasted jacket' and the 'smile' (figure 22). Bringing Berlusconi's image to the fore serves also to index the political and socio-economic context, or, in Kurtz's words, the 'situation', the 'place', and the 'state of things' against which he wants 'to fight together with you'. Finally, Kurtz describes the 'vision' that reveals the symbolic

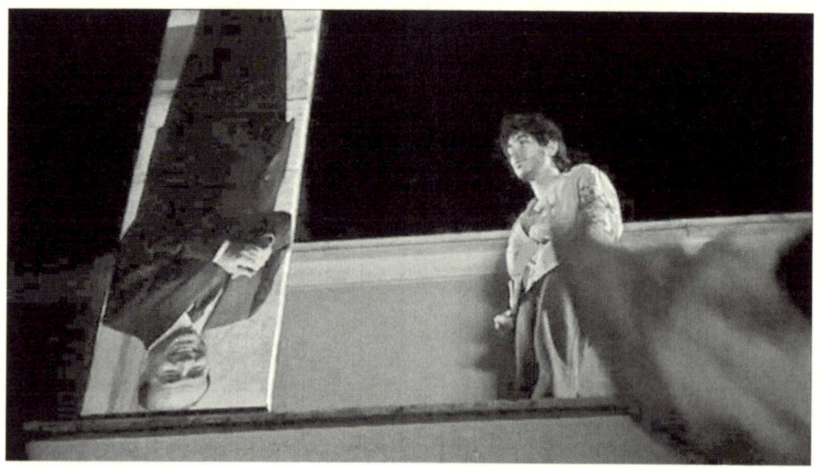

Figure 22. Kurtz uncovers the poster of Berlusconi before the speech.

substance of Berlusconi: in his hallucination, Berlusconi is 'the tip of the iceberg, the spring of the river of aridity in which we all are drowning', and the 'undisputed symbol of this age without virtue'.

Even if it is pompous and rhetorical, Kurtz's speech is clear and philosophically founded. On one hand, he accuses himself and his generation of being nihilistic and individualistic; on the other hand, he identifies in Berlusconi the source of their problem and proposes a collective solution. More precisely, his proposal is an attempt to create a collective scapegoat. According to René Girard, it is through collective processes of scapegoating, that he calls 'scapegoating mechanism', that societies work and cultures are created (222). Italian society participated in this mechanism, for example, with the killing of Mussolini and, thirty years later, with that of Aldo Moro. While it is a historical fact that the partisans killed Mussolini on April 25, 1945 and the Red brigades killed Aldo Moro on May 9, 1978, nonetheless, these killings have been used by Italian society for collective processes and discourses of political regeneration.

One final note on the film's original title in English; *Shooting Silvio*. It has ambivalent meanings — 'to gun down' and 'to film'. This deliberate ambivalence sets the stage for the assassination narrative as well as a meta-film narrative, or the film about making a film on Berlusconi, which, as we have seen, is a common motif in the films on Berlusconi. One more time, the viewer is asked to see the characters, their motivations, and their story, through the filter of Berlusconi's persona, which is the intended center of the representation. Also the emptiness and absurdity of most of Kurtz's friends, a few adult characters — the notary public, the waiter, and the secretary — the journalist Marco Travaglio, and the archival footage of Berlusconi are all to be understood as parts of Berlusconi's semiotic universe.

The Failure of Contingencies: Ops… Ho ammazzato Berlusconi!

The third film that needs to be discussed in the *in morte* corpus is *Ops… Ho ammazzato Berlusconi!*. This film uses a comedic register to stage a paradoxical contrast between the powerful political body of Berlusconi and that of the film protagonist. An original adaptation from Andrea Saleri's novel *L'omicidio Berlusconi* (2003), *Ops…* is a black comedy pivoting around the life of Matteo (Alberto Bognanni), a good-natured and modest high school teacher married to Livia (Sabrina Paravicini), a feminist left-wing activist. The film is set at the time of the 2001 national election. After Berlusconi's victory, the progressive electorate is shaken and Livia is especially upset because a friend informs her that Matteo, a convinced left-wing voter, secretly voted for Berlusconi. Matteo is unable to explain why he made this decision and Livia is infuriated. She leaves the house in the middle of the night, but is hit by the errant piece of an airplane which just exploded in the air, and dies. A few days after the funeral, Matteo, overcome by feelings of guilt and sadness, goes out for a car ride in a rainy night and accidentally crashes into a man. After clumsy attempts to help the man, Matteo in fact kills him with a car jack. Matteo buries the corpse, but when he discovers that the man is Silvio Berlusconi, he unburies him, puts him in the freezer (figures 23 and 24) and goes to the police and confesses to murder. Nobody believes Matteo's rather implausible story. After all, Berlusconi seems to be alive and well since he appears in television all day long. Matteo, frustrated at not being believed, decides to get rid of the corpse, but is kidnapped by three men from Berlusconi's staff, Cesare, Gianni, and Giuliano (reminiscent of Cesare Previti Gianni, Letta, and Giuliano Ferrara). The three men tell him that the Berlusconi who appears in television is a well-trained double and offer Matteo twenty million euros and a one-way flight to Cuba in exchange for the corpse. Matteo accepts, seeking assistance of his friend Gaetano (Andrea Roncato), who is a professional nurse, in transporting the corpse. The meeting to deliver the body turns out to be a trap, where Gaetano is killed. Matteo goes back home, buries the corpse in his garden again, and shuts himself up in his house.

After living some time in a sort of paranoid segregation, he finally loses his mind and buries himself alongside with Berlusconi's body. In his last words and speaking at the camera, he confesses his sense of guilt for Livia's death.

The semiosis of Berlusconi's body is the narrative center of this black comedy. The film focuses almost exclusively on the murder, manipulation, and elimination of the corpse, offering the opportunity to play with various degrees of comic modes and cinematic genres. The unintended killing, for example, takes several minutes, and focuses on visual details that are characteristic of zom-

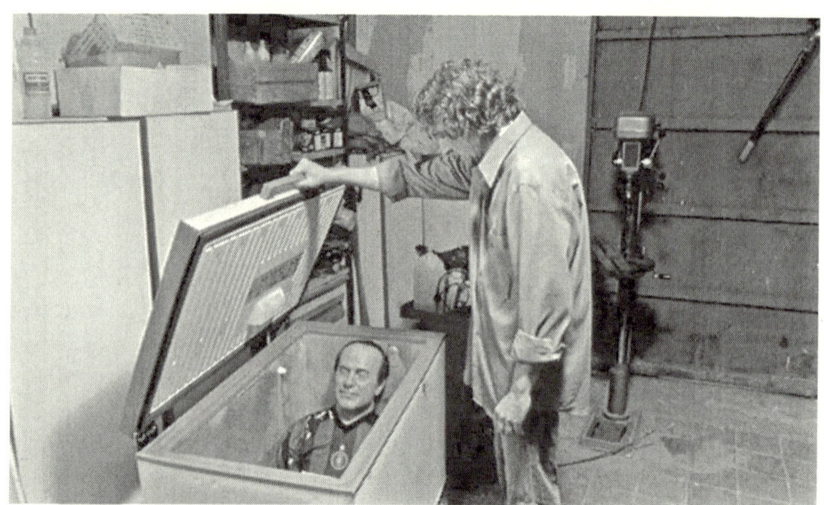

Figure 23. Matteo contemplates Berlusconi's corpse in his freezer.

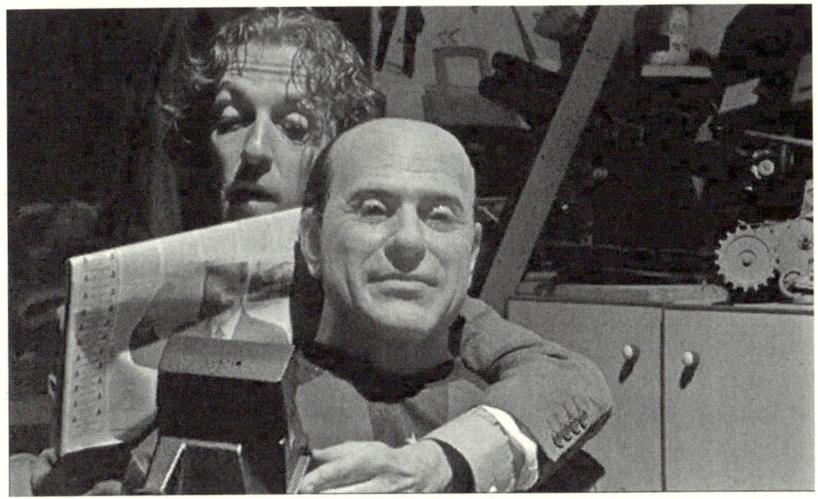

Figure 24. Matteo takes a picture of the corpse with his polaroid to prove that Berlusconi is alive.

bie and horror films: Matteo is seen against the background of the rainy night while a close up of the arm of the (still) unknown man slowly moves in agony in the foreground; then a few close ups of the man's face altered by horrific details alternate with long shots of the dark background. The comic modes in which Matteo manipulates the corpse unfold according to an interesting duality. As soon as Matteo finds out its identity, the corpse becomes a cumbersome presence that reminds him of his double responsibility — ethical and political — for killing an individual and assassinating a politician. In other words, he becomes responsible for both a biological and a symbolic assassination. The comic situations stem from the paradoxical opposition between the biological body and the body politic, and this tension is reflected in the style of a comedy of errors, with contradictory or false statements, exchange of identities, masquerades, and misunderstandings, which make the film funny and clever.

The duality intrinsic in the opposition between biological body and body politic complicates this black comedy of errors. It actually derives from the notion of 'the king's two bodies' theorized by Ernst H. Kantorowicz, which claims that the sovereign has two bodies: the biological one, which is subject to illness, infirmity, and death, and the mystical one, which symbolizes the abstractions of regality and powers, transcends the limitations of the biological body and remains as an eternal indication of its own function in the world. *Ops...* establishes this duality in a mechanical and literal way. On one hand there is a murdered corpse which can be buried and forgotten, while on the other hand there is a body politic, an abstraction — a zombie, according to the conventions of the genre — that cannot be killed.

4.
THE NON-FICTIONAL BODY POLITIC

Citizen Kane was a 'flea', a nothing, in comparison with Berlusconi.
Giovanni Sartori

From 2001 to date, there has been a proliferation of documentary films on Silvio Berlusconi (Castelli 2011: 223-24). At least fourteen films have been produced in Italy or targeted to Italian audiences, while four more were produced for international audiences and shot in English or French. Below is the complete corpus, in chronological order, with production information:[1]

2001 *Il più migliore al mondo* (The Bestest of the World). Aurelio Grimaldi. Gruppo Pasquino. Italy.*

2003 *Citizen Berlusconi*. Andrea Cairola, Susan Gray. Stefilm/ WNET. USA/Italy/Germany/Finland.

2003 *Sua Maestà Silvio Berlusconi* (Your Majesty Silvio Berlusconi). Stéphane Bentura. Capa Presse TV Paris. France.

2004 *Lilli e il cavaliere* (Lilli and the *Cavaliere*). Caterina Borelli. Anonymous Productions. Italy.*

2005 *Quando c'era Silvio* (When There Was Silvio). Beppe Cremagnani, Enrico Deaglio. Luben. Italy.

2005 *Grazie Berlusconi!* (Thanks Berlusconi!) Fulvia Alberti. Article Z. France.

2005 *Viva Zapatero* (Long Live Zapatero!) Sabina Guzzanti. Lucky Red/Sciocco. Italy.

2006 *Berlusconi, Affaire Mondadori*. Mosco Boucault. ARTE Francia/Zex. France.

---

1   The list of documentaries is presented in this chapter for readability, but it is also included in the corpus listed in the Appendix. The * indicates the documentaries that are not currently available in any form.

2006 *In un altro paese* (In Another Country). Marco Turco. Doclab/Artline Films/RAI 3/France 2.

2009 *Videocracy. Basta apparire.* (Videocracy. Appearing Is Enough.) Erik Gandini. Atmo AB/Zentropa. Sweden.

2010 *Draquila. L'Italia che trema* (Draquila. Italy Trembles). Sabina Guzzanti. Sciocco. Italy.

2010 *Le dame e il cavaliere* (The Dames and the Knight). Francesca Gnetti, Franco Fracassi. Telemaco. Italy.

2010 *Sorelle d'Italia* (Sisters of Italy). Lorenzo Buccella, Vito Robbiani. Media TREE/Amka. Switzerland.

2011 *Silvio Forever.* Roberto Faenza and Filippo Macelloni. Ad Hoc Film. Italy.

2011 *Italy: Love It or Leave It.* Gustav Hofer, Luca Ragazzi. hiq/NDR/WDR/RAITre. Italy.

2012 *S.B. Io lo conoscevo bene* (S.B. I Knew Him Well). Giacomo Durzi, Giovanni Fasanella. Kinesis. Italy.

2012 *Girlfriend in a Coma.* Bill Emmot and Annalisa Pira. Springshot. U.K.

2014. *La trattativa* (The Pact). Sabina Guzzanti. Secol Superbo e Sciocco. Italy.

While this is an impressive list, these films have barely circulated in traditional venues. Those produced for an Italian audience were shown mainly in specialized circuits, such as documentary festivals, or were marketed directly to DVD. Only a few of these films were broadcast on television, but for a very limited time. The case of *Il più migliore al mondo* (Grimaldi 2001) is particularly striking. It was broadcast from *La7* in October 2005, then it completely disappeared and now it is impossible to find.[2] *Silvio Forever* (Faenza and Macelloni 2011) was released in 108 movie theaters in March 2011 — an impressive count at the time — but was broadcast on *La7* only in September of the same year. Public television did not even allow the streaming of the trailer. *S.B. Io lo conoscevo bene* (Durzi and Fasanella 2012), which appeared in the 2012 International Film Festival of Rome, where it received positive feedback, but was never shown on television or in other public venues after that. *Le dame e il cavaliere* (Gnetti and Fracassi 2010) was neither released in theaters nor distributed as a DVD,

---

2   In this regard see the introductory chapter of this book, n. 9, p. 18.

and it is only available online. *Videocracy* (Gandini 2009) appeared first at the 2009 International Film Festival of Venice and was subsequently distributed in a limited amount of copies. It was finally broadcast from *La7* in 2011 in the talk show *Film Evento*.

The productions targeting international audiences — including *Citizen Berlusconi* (Cairola and Gray 2003), *Sua Maestà Silvio Berlusconi* (Bentura 2003), *Berlusconi, Affaire Mondadori* (Boucault 2006), and *Girlfriend in a Coma* (Emmott and Piras 2012) — were not released in theaters in Italy. However, they are currently all accessible online or as DVDs, with Italian subtitles.[3]

Despite the difficulty of distribution, thanks to social media platforms such as Facebook and YouTube, these documentary features reached at least a part of their intended audiences. Interestingly, the new models of circulation facilitated by contemporary 'networked culture' have endowed these films with the characteristic of 'spreadabilty' (Jenkins 2013), and with greater potential to generate political opposition.

What is particularly interesting in this corpus is the variety of tropes and themes that the documentaries on Berlusconi interrogate. They explore the figure of Silvio Berlusconi (or *Berlusconismo*) from different angles, including gender, media, business, organized crime, and other social perspectives. Because of this variety, the modes of observation also vary and include investigative and political documentary, satiric impersonation, and meta-film.[4] Yet, in most of these documentaries the narrative nucleus remains Berlusconi's theatrical, plasticized, erotized, and mediated body. It is significant that, over the years, documentaries on Berlusconi continue to be based on similar iconographic material and oppositional discourses. Discussing the idea of the feminization of Berlusconi, Catherine O'Rawe argues that tropes of men

---

3   As it happened with other antagonistic productions, such as Berardo Carboni's *Shooting* Silvio, the internationally produced documentaries were not released in theaters or problems arose that prevented them from being released. The premiere of Piras's *Girlfriend in a Coma* was scheduled at the Maxxi on February 13, 2013, but the Ministry of Culture ordered that it be rescheduled until after the elections. British journalist Bill Emmott, who co-authored the documentary, accused the Ministry of 'censorship' (*La Repubblica* 2013).

4   For a comprehensive reading on Sabina Guzzanti's impersonation of Silvio Berlusconi, see Clare Watters' study, *Being Berlusconi* (2011).

in crisis can contribute to 'recentering hegemonic masculinity' (7). I would add that the obsessive focus on the Prime Minister's body and the amusement that originates from it could in fact be a way to reaffirm his 'playful image' as positive and empowering.

From the Political Outsider to the 'Category of the Spirit'

Because the documentaries are so numerous, I selectively chose to discuss only a few works produced from 2001 (the year of the first documentary) to 2012, which focus on Berlusconi's political trajectory.[5] They are significant as a group because they trace the political parable of *Il Cavaliere* in interesting ways and raise meaningful questions in their heterogeneity. Bill Nichols reminds us that documentary films are characterized by 'fluidity', which 'makes for a dynamic, evolving form' (2010 chap. 6 Kindle ebook). In the case of the documentaries on Berlusconi, 'fluidity' is a necessary concept to make sense of the variety of approaches that we as the 'interpretive communities' (Fish 1982: 168) find in front of us.

The first documentaries made on Berlusconi as a political leader are dominated by male figures and urgently investigate the political outsider and media tycoon. They follow the 'expository mode' insofar as they emphasize 'the verbal commentary and an argumentative logic', according to Nichols's broad definition (chap. 6 Kindle ebook). Some of the voice-overs use a didactic and omniscient tone, while others have a more casual, conversational disposition. For example, *Citizen Berlusconi* (Cairola and Gray 2003), an episode produced by PBS for the *Wide Angle* series, is overtly didactic. It starts with a rhetorical question that the viewers supposedly can answer by watching the film: 'Who is Silvio Berlusconi? He is funny. He is rich. And he is powerful. But is he good for democracy?' (*Citizen*) The audience is invited to follow the voice-over exposition and the subsequent interview of the journalist Alexander Stille, who provides an authoritative

---

5   The *Italian Frame* is conceived as a series of short volumes for quick consultation. The space limits made it necessary to restrict the analysis to a few films.

perspective on the problematic career of Berlusconi. As Castelli points out, the PBS series *Wide Angle* normally focused on ordinary people. The Berlusconi episode was an unusual exception to that format and served to put Berlusconi in perspective, 'deglamorizing and demystifying' him (225).

In the French productions *Sua maestà Silvio Berlusconi* (Bentura 2003) and *Berlusconi, Affaire Mondadori* (Boucault 2006), the voice-over plays a less relevant part. Instead, at the foreground are a number of interviews in which only the interviewees speak. Targeted to a French audience, they focus on issues related to Berlusconi in the French context, such as the controversies around *LaCinq* (the first privately-owned free television channel in France created by Berlusconi) and the French ramifications of the Mondadori Affaire.

The investigative tone and journalistic information that one finds in *Citizen*, *Sua Maestà*, and *Affaire* are central in *Quando c'era Silvio* (Cremagnani and Deaglio 2005), where, again, an authoritative male voice-over narrates the complex history of Berlusconi, from his beginnings as an entrepreneur in Milan through the 'descent into the field' in 1994 and his political escalation up to 2005. The voice-over is accompanied by a long 'cartographic' sequence, which is reminiscent of a fascist war-time *cinegiornale* (cine news) and conjures up the image of a military march through Italy (the drums are in fact audible in the background) with sinister political implications for the figure of Berlusconi and his political leadership (figure 25). Similar scenes repeat throughout the film. To emphasize the end of Berlosconi's political experience, the voice-over uses the *passato remoto* (simple past), a tense that is used in Italian to narrate historical events that took place in a distant past. This stylistic choice relegates Berlusconi and *Berlusconismo* to a remote past with no relevance or connections to the present time. It sounds surreal but in 2008, only three years after the film's release, Berlusconi was elected again. The archival footage, animations, and pictures that accompany the narration also offer a bizarre but scary portrait of Berlusconi. This not only contributes to his demonization, but also draws attention to discreet aspects of his formidable personality. In this documentary, archival footage of interviews while he was in office, with a variety of people from the economic and political world, including the

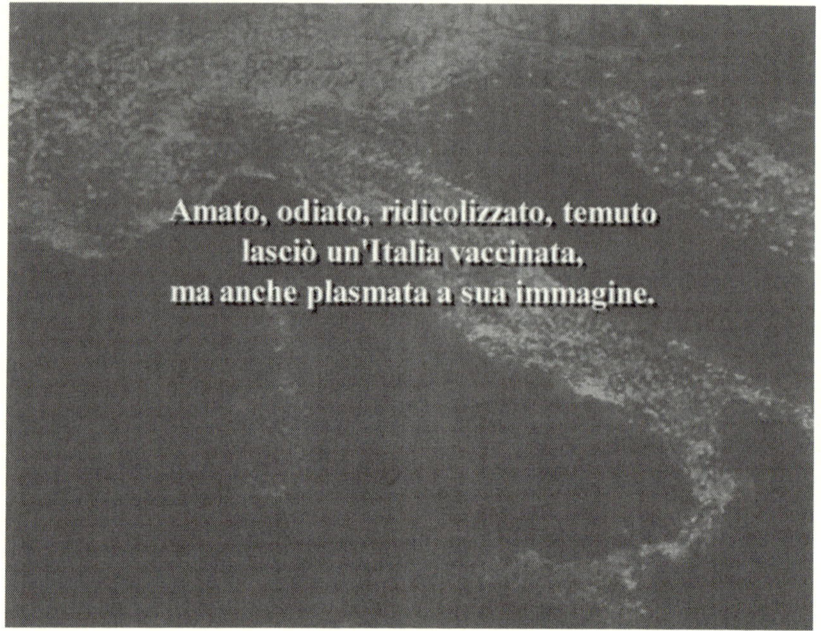

Figure 25. The March on Italy, with the voice-over speaking of Berlusconi
in the *passato remoto*.

Falck family (leaders of the Italian steel industry during the economic boom), Judge Falcone (assassinated by the Mafia in 1992), and former Judge Di Pietro (one of the Milanese prosecutors of the *Mani Pulite* (Clean Hands) operation), reflect the authoritative oppositional discourse that has become mainstream in Italian media. Other oppositional figures in this feature are Judge Antonio Ingroia, a prosecutor in one of Berlusconi's many trials, and comedian Daniele Luttazzi, who was notoriously fired publicly by Berlusconi for his non-conformist positions.

The archival footage, used abundantly in *Quando c'era Silvio*, introduces some sequences and images that consistently appear in other documentaries and narrative films and assist in capturing the semiosis of Berlusconi in cinema that is the basis of this book. One of these sequences is the Strasbourg 'kapo' accident that also appears in Moretti's *Il Caimano* and in Berardi's *Shooting Silvio*. Another particularly significant scene is the visit to the mausoleum, which is a monumental grave in Berlusconi's villa in Arcore, Milan. Berlusconi commissioned a sculptor, Pietro Cascella, for the job. The voice-over presents the mausoleum as a mysterious building with masonic symbols and gossips about its potential use as a cryogenic facility, implying that Berlusconi is planning to preserve his body from death. The voice-over compares the mausoleum to that of Tutankhamun, Stalin, Evita Peron, Mao Zedong, Ho Chi Min, and Kim Il-Sung. This comparison clearly evokes the symbolism of the 'king's two bodies', but in such an exaggerated manner that it makes Berlusconi's body a caricature.[6] On the other hand, Stalin, Marx, and Mussolini are also mentioned several times in the film to highlight Berlusconi's legitimization of the Neofascist Party and the rehabilitation of the historical role of Mussolini. These references also point to Berlusconi's repositioning towards ultraconservative positions.

An additional layer frames the 'historical' war-like presentation of *Quando c'era Silvio*: a 'once-upon-a-time' narrative that evokes a symbolic fairy-tale-esque dimension. Actress Lella Costa opens and closes the film by reading a passage from Collodi's *Pinocchio* that describes the *Omino di burro* (Little Butter Man, or the Coachman) — clearly a metaphor for *Il Cavaliere* — riding the carriage to the *Paese dei balocchi* (Land of Toys), or Italy. (figure 26). This narrative, which suggests the lack of maturity of Berlusconi and his constituency, reduces Berlusconi's power to the fantasy summoned in the mind of an infantile, ridiculous man.

The most powerful documentary on the iconography of Berlusconi's body is *Silvio Forever* (Faenza and Macelloni 2011), which encapsulates the themes discussed so far and shows the permeability of the boundary between fact and fiction. In this film, the iconic images and sequences from previous documentaries fill the screen and the *bunga bunga* women eventually occupy the stage, destabilizing the prevailing investigative narrative and focusing the viewer's attention on the sexual scandals involving Berlusconi (figure 27). Berlusconi's body is the physical and symbolic core of *Silvio Forever*, which is a montage of archival footage and still pictures of Berlusconi himself. During the opening credits of *Silvio Forever* the camera pivots around Berlusconi's

---

6   See this book, pp. 18-19 and 75-76.

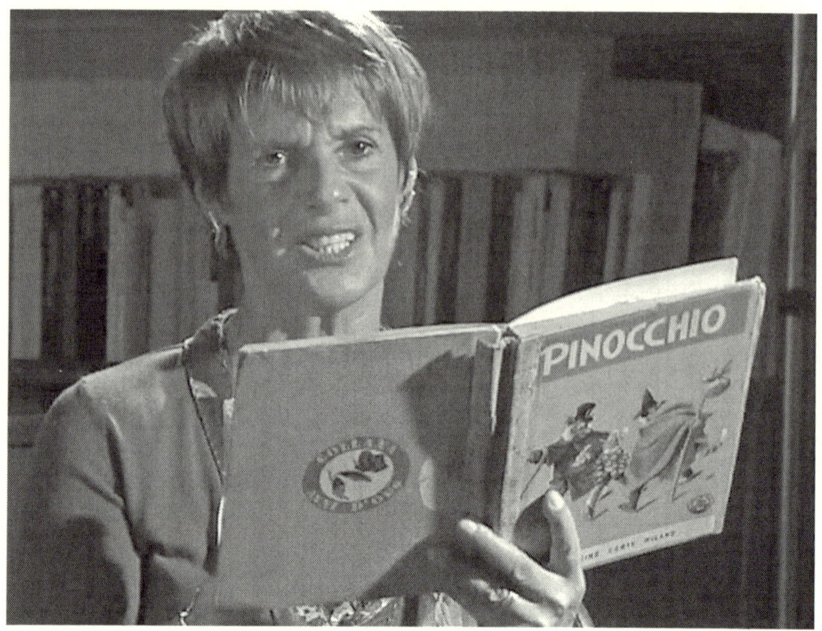

Figure 26. Lella Costa reads aloud the story of the Little Butter Man
from *Pinocchio*.

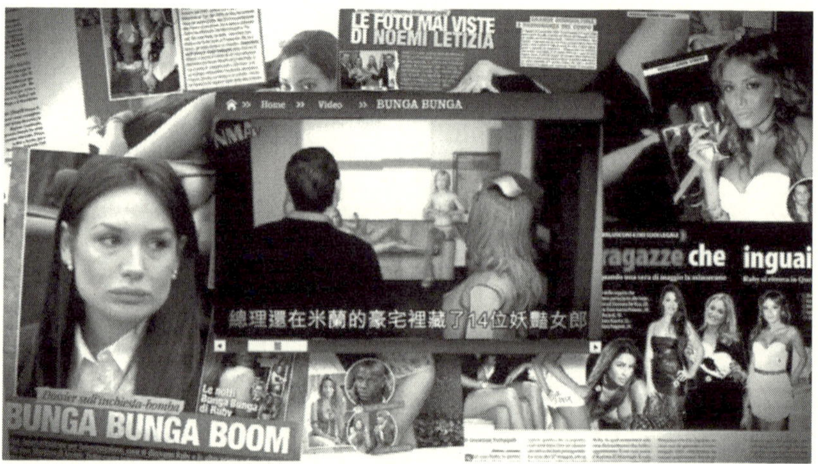

Figure 27. The *bunga bunga* images.

body from multiple perspectives and across time (figure 28). The third-person voice-over of the 'expository' mode has disappeared and is replaced by the voice of Berlusconi himself, drawn from original footage or imitated by actor Neri Marcorè. The investigative mode and the oppositional experts presenting from a didactic perspective have disappeared as well. The lack of mediation shows how the 'semiotic excess' (Fiske 1986: 403) of Berlusconi's body has endowed the narrative with a symbolic surplus that does not need external explanations. In *Silvio Forever*, Berlusconi's body is an autonomous narrative device that produces its own meanings. Unlike any other film on Berlusconi, comedians, politicians, scholars and journalists — such as Roberto Benigni, Indro Montanelli, Umberto Eco, Andrea Camilleri, Beppe Grillo, and Nichi Vendola — appear through found footage. In this way, they too become part of the spectacle, alongside 'mamma Rosa' (Berlusconi's mother), and are deprived of any authoritative position. The manner in which the documentary is framed shows its narrative force. 'Mamma Rosa' opens the film talking about her son as a publicly recognized benefactor: 'he is so good, so generous [*pause*] I think that everyone says that' (*Silvio Forever*). The grotesque finale juxtaposes footage from a theatrical assassination of Julius Caesar — alluding to Berlusconi's political body —

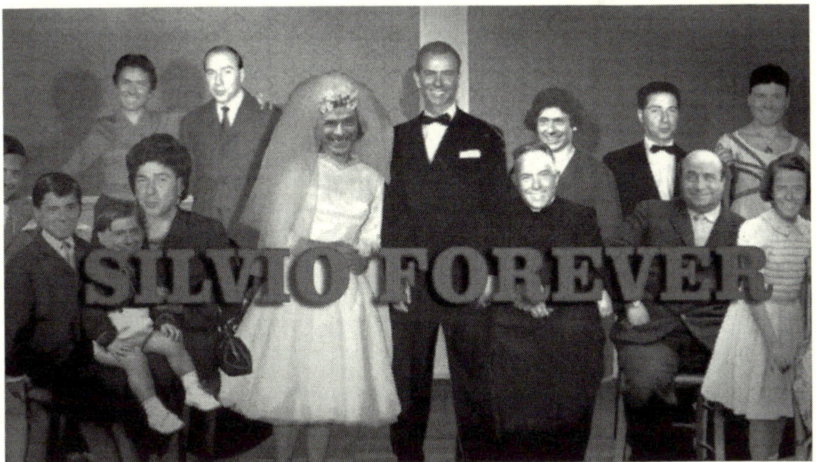

Figure 28. The opening credits of *Silvio Forever*.

with Berlusconi's voice telling a joke about discussing his position as 'president of heaven' with God.

The last documentary on Berlusconi's political trajectory is *S.B. Io lo conoscevo bene* (Durzi and Fasanella 2012). In this film, Berlusconi's body is spectralized. Beyond the iconic images and archival footage that are routinely used in most documentaries, *S.B.* shows some interesting innovations. The narrative is based on interviews of former friends, who were close to Berlusconi during his 'heroic' entrepreneurial phase, but then had negative experiences with him. Just to mention a few, these 'friends' include: former Socialist mayor of Milan Paolo Pillitteri, implicated in the 'Clean Hands' anti-corruption operation; Vincenzo Dotti and Stefania Ariosto, two key figures of the so-called 'Segrate war' for the control of the Mondadori holding; journalist and former minister of one of Berlusconi's governments, Giuliano Ferrara; and Paolo Cirino Pomicino, the former Christian Democratic minister of one of Giulio Andreotti's governments. The confessional tone of the interviewees and their historical insights distinguish the documentary from other similar works. While the focus of the film is still Berlusconi, his body is removed from the stage, both physically and symbolically, and the viewer has time and space to listen to and think about the interviewees' self-reflections. It is as if the *fracasso* had finally quieted because Berlusconi's political season is coming to an end. However, it is significant that in the final sequences the camera moves across empty, silent rooms and hallways, while one of the old friends, Cirino Pomicino, speaks of a sense of 'reordering', and of *Berlusconismo* as a 'category of the spirit' (*S.B. Io lo conoscevo bene*). This finale seems to imply that the removal of Berlusconi's persona — albeit bringing the old 'order' back — will not erase the cultural and political change brought about by *Berlusconismo* in contemporary Italy. As Ida Dominijanni points out, Berlusconi will continue to be a 'spectral presence', that of a 'leader legally dethroned who will not stop looming' over us (2014a 150).

5.
BERLUSCONI *POST-MORTEM*

Tutti noi sfioriamo brandelli di Storia di continuo.
Francesco Piccolo

The Grotesque Knight: Belluscone. Una storia siciliana.

In a private interview given during the post-production of *Belluscone*, Franco Maresco explained that he was experiencing a profound 'existential crisis' stemming from the realization that 'digital trash' and an 'immense amount of shit' had inundated Italy and the world (2013). He claimed that the barbaric sub-human world staged in *Cinico TV* in the 1990s had materialized in the 'monstrous drift' of Berlusconi's Italy (Ibid.). Feeling 'sucked into a vortex of defeat', he believed that cinema, as he knew it, could not exist anymore and his reason d'être as an artist and intellectual 'mediator' ended forever (Ibid.). He confessed that if he could, he would 'retire' and 'remove' himself from the public stage. (Ibid.). Maresco's film *Belluscone* (2014) conveys this sense of apocalypse, isolation and failure. In fact, alongside with *Il ritorno di Cagliostro* (2003) and *Io sono Tony Scott* (2010), it completes 'a sort of trilogy of failure' (*Il Manifesto* 2015). It also marks a breaking point in Maresco's artistic path and professional life because it takes shape during the painful separation from his former colleague and friend, Daniele Ciprì, and the bankruptcy of their production company, *Cinico Cinema.*
Stylistically, *Belluscone* stands out in Maresco's (and Ciprì's) film production as an eccentric and complex work blurring the boundaries between a narrative, documentary, auteurist and metacinematic film. It is not staged in the 'empty streets littered with mounds of indistinguishable trash' and 'barren and lifeless'

landscapes with blurred and hazy horizons typical of Ciprì's and Maresco's works (Seger 2012: 265, 269). Quite the opposite: it unfolds as an apparently absurdist mix of excerpts from newsreels, archival footage, staged and street interviews, shows from local channels and Fininvest networks, and performances by the so-called *neomelodici* singers. These excerpts create a composite structure consisting of obsessive 'returning circularities' (Ghezzi 2014) pivoting around three main narratives. First, Silvio Berlusconi's trajectory from his alleged relationship with the Mafia up to his resignation in 2011 and his replacement by his Democratic opponent, Matteo Renzi, in 2013. Second, the life and deeds of the *neomelodici* singers' impresario and Mafioso, Ciccio Mira, and the Sicilian world that surrounds him. And third, the tortuous story of the making of the film, narrated as a work in progress by cinema critic and Maresco's friend, Tatti Sanguineti.[1] Each 'circle' frames the other ones as a paradigm of failure. In fact, in Maresco's words, *Belluscone* presents

> three poor men's parallel lives, the story of their failures: Silvio Berlusconi's political failure, the failure of the *neomelodici* singers' agent, Ciccio Mira, put in a corner by his own creatures, who seem to be coming from an invasion of body snatchers. And my failure as a director.' (Ulivi 2014)

Notwithstanding his declaration of artistic self-defeat, these three apparently incompatible narratives are skillfully united by Maresco's directorial voice. He interviews Ciccio Mira, the *neomelodici* singers, and people partying in street fairs to explore their relationship with the Mafia as well as Berlusconi. His off-screen narration provides a critical commentary that connects the lumpenproletariat of the *Quartiere Brancaccio* in Palermo to the bourgeois Milanese milieu of Berlusconi's story. In other words, his narrative spans from micro- to macro-historical frameworks and from archaic communities to contemporary mediated landscapes. An unsettling sense of disproportion unifies this multiplicity creating a grotesque reality that invests not only its main

---

1   Sanguineti also participates in Moretti's *Il caimano,* where he plays himself at the screening of Bruno Bonomo's (fake) B-movie *Cataratte* (Cataracts), the sequence that opens Moretti's film.

object of representation, that is, Berlusconi's persona and his *storia siciliana*, but also the over-mediated reality of contemporary Italy and the cinematic language itself.

In my interview, Maresco explained that with *Belluscone* he intended to document the Sicilian genesis of Silvio Berlusconi's climb to power. He claimed that the subtitle *Una storia siciliana* (A Sicilian Story) aimed at 'correcting' the title and the narrative of the glamorizing pamphlet *Una storia Italiana* (An Italian Story, 2001) that Berlusconi mailed to all Italian households for the 2001 election (Maresco). In fact, *Belluscone* highlights the most controversial points in the entrepreneurial details of the pamphlet's biography, such as the unclear beginning of his career in the construction business, his alleged search for Mafia protection from kidnapping in the 1970s, the financial support supposedly received from Mafia boss Stefano Bontate, the 'descent into the field' in 1994, his evolution to a spectacularized tycoon and politician, his resignation from office in 2011, and the post-Berlusconi Italy.

However, *Belluscone* is far from being a political biopic in the vein of Italian cinema of *impegno*. Maresco's satyric approach creates a hybrid film that is purposefully discontinuous and inconclusive. In spite of an engaging beginning that promises to dig into the true story of Berlusconi's ascent to power and to reveal his ties to Sicily, the investigative impulse gets lost in the making, and the declared intention to produce an orthodox documentary grounded in the mainstream critical discourse on Berlusconi is discarded. In fact, Maresco's interviews of Berlusconi's most noted opponents, such as journalist Marco Travaglio and magistrate Antonio Ingroia, (who have relevant roles in several films on Berlusconi) are relegated to extras in the movie's DVD. More importantly, Maresco's interaction with Ciccio Mira and his narration of Berlusconi's career are interrupted abruptly after the first ten minutes of the film, when Tatti Sanguineti enters the frame and symbolically stops a tape recorder playing Maresco's voice. According to a film-within-the-film logic, Sanguineti informs the viewers that the director disappeared while working on *Belluscone*. He explains that he is leaving for Sicily to find his 'fugitive' (*Belluscone*) friend and give him support in his investigation and the making of the film. From this point on, the plot follows Sanguineti's journey trailing Maresco's footprints, and

Belluscone's third narrative 'circle' takes shape as a metacinematic narration of the director's catastrophic attempt to tell the *storia siciliana* of Berlusconi.

In Sicily, Sanguineti talks with Maresco's assistants and consultants, who point him to hours of discarded footage, of which only a small part is shown to the viewer. Most of the clips that are included in the film through the fictional recounting of Sanguineti center on the Sicilians' infatuation with Berlusconi and on his local young bards, that is, the *neomelodici* singers, particularly Salvatore 'Erik' De Castro (figure 29), from Villa Grazia (Palermo), and Vittorio Ricciardi (figure 30), from Naples. The vintage, black-and-white hero of this plot-line is Ciccio Mira (figure 31), who presents himself as both a showman and a nostalgic wiseman from the old-guard Mafia that killed only when necessary, according to an inflexible honor code. Mira controls the organization of *neomelodici*'s concerts and leads a show broadcast by TBS, a local TV channel, which entertains the viewers with exhibitions of *neomelodici* and *bunga-bunga* dances. During the show, Mira candidly coordinates exchanges of messages between inmates, that the locals respectfully call *ospiti dello stato* (State's guests), and their families.

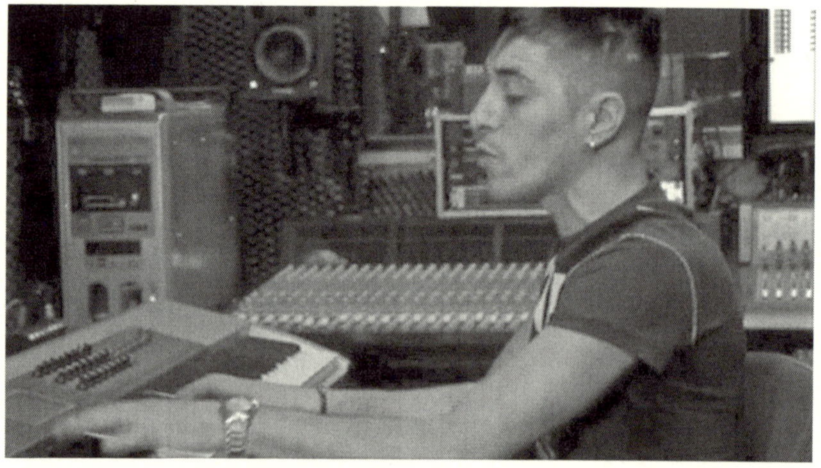

Figure 29. Salvatore 'Erik' De Castro is performing the song 'Voglio conoscere Berlusconi'.

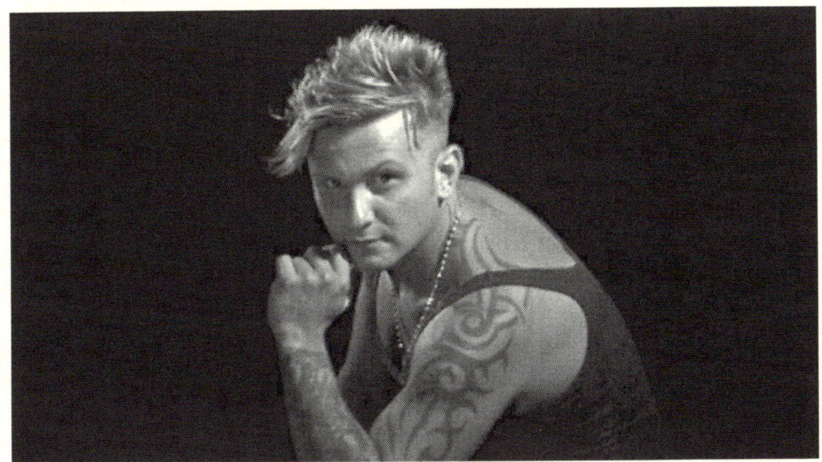

Figure 30. Vittorio Ricciardi poses for the interview with Franco Maresco in *Belluscone.*

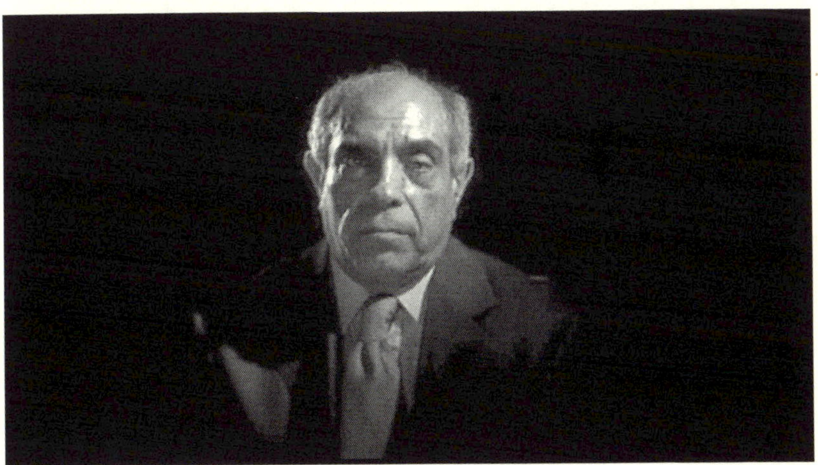

Figure 31. Ciccio Mira during the interview with Franco Maresco. Mira is in black and white throughout the film.

In *Belluscone*, Mira acts as a tragicomic guide, who introduces Maresco to local characters and places, and gives him cryptic hints on the Palermo Mafia context using the *omertà* code. In Sanguineti's words, Mira is Maresco's one more 'pray to harpoon' as he is a 'former barber, a former singer, and an impresario of emergent talents' (*Belluscone*), that is, Berlusconi's Sicilian lower-class and mafioso alter ego. This parallelism is implied by the juxtaposition of the two men's storylines and becomes more explicit around the center of the film, when Berlusconi, from archival footage, speaks of himself as a *qualunquista* and of his idea that the government is useless, indeed, harmful to his business. Suggesting interchangeability between the two men, this scene transitions with a wipe cut to Maresco's interview of Mira: 'What is your concept of the State, Ciccio?', asks Maresco. Mira answers with a laconic, 'Nothing, it's nothing' (Ibid.).

The correlation between Mira and Berlusconi — and their respective social environments — encapsulates the trope of the grotesque double body dominating the film's plot-line, mise-en-scène and montage. It is through the idea of a grotesque collision between the comic and tragic spheres (De Gaetano 1999: 7) that Maresco dramatizes his apocalyptic vision of the world, which sees Western culture and Sicilian society in particular, as 'irredeemable' (St. Ours 199). The landscapes of Ciprì's and Maresco's 'classic' works, namely, *Cinico* TV, *Lo zio di Brooklyn* (1995) and *Totò che visse due volte* (1998), are populated with 'low-lifes in a world where nothing really happens [...] string[ing] together sequences that defy our sensori-motor expectations' (ibid.). This 'sub-humanity' (De Gaetano 1999: 109) produces a sense of '"monstrous" grotesque' through 'hyperboles with no return' and 'deformed bodies' (25). In *Belluscone*, there is a different form of monstrosity, which is socially and historically contextualized in the interconnections between the Sicilian world and Berlusconi. The grotesque is revealed through the disproportional juxtaposition of low and high, the tribe and the individual, the South and the North, the *neomelodica* music and the Mafia, the proletariat and the bourgeoisie, and, most importantly, the secrecy of *omertà* and the *fracasso* of mediated reality. This grotesque duality literally shows the 'disaggregation' of the Italian social body (De Gaetano 1999: 27) and expands to the metacinematic language and apparatus that surround the narration. The faulty analog equipment that Maresco's crew seems to use, unsuccessfully, to record his useless interview of Marcello Dell'Utri sitting on a hyperbolic throne of power (figure 32), is emblematic.

There is a revealing moment in the film, which emphasizes how the grotesque degradation of the reality is also reflected in language. It is journalist Pino Maniaci's comment on the song 'Voglio conoscere Berlusconi' (I Want to Meet Berlusconi) created by singer Erik to honor Berlusconi. In the film, Maniaci helps Maresco interview local mafiosi and mediates between Maresco, Erik, and Vittorio on a question of copyright over the song. He then meets Sanguineti, who is still seeking information about his friend. Maniaci leads Sanguineti to Villa Grazia and explains that Erik composed

> a song on Berlusconi to *sort of singing his feats…* and we wondered… right here… why in this area, which was, so to speak, Stefano Bontate's *kingdom* in the 1970s… because we are in Villa Grazia here… do you know what Villa Grazia is, what it represents? […] Villa Grazia was Stefano Bontate's *kingdom*, exactly where, right around here, he was killed in the 1980s. So it's a very… very well known area. (*Belluscone.* Added emphasis)

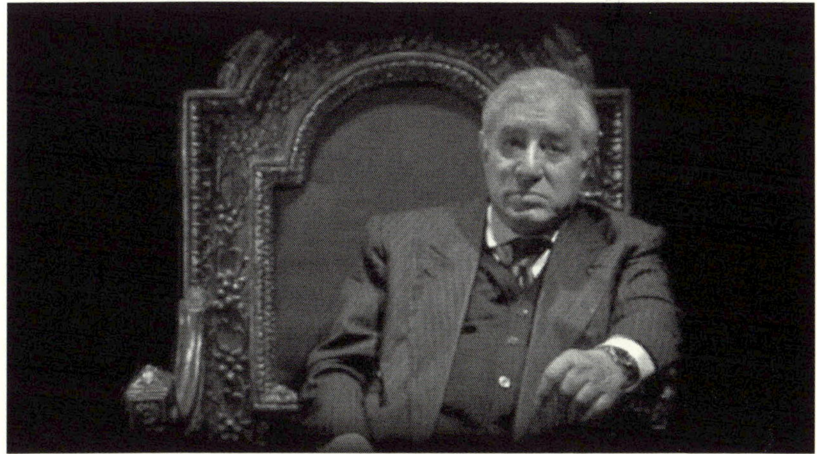

Figure 32. Marcello Dell'Utri on the throne during the interview with Maresco.

While implying that both Erik and Berlusconi have something to share within Bontate's territory, Maniaci's language is ambivalent. First of all, it betrays deference for the spheres of power that *Il Cavaliere* and Bontate respectively represent. His expression 'singing his feats' (in Italian: 'cantarne le gesta') literally evokes the *chanson de geste,* adopting an exaggerated epic register and endowing *Il Cavaliere* with a mythological aura — although compensating with 'un po'' (sort of). Insisting on the semantic field of epic, Maniaci defines Villa Grazia as Bontate's 'kingdom', emphasizing the boss's sovereign power in the area. On the other hand, Maniaci's insistent use of deixis ('here… in this area… Villa Grazia… right here') and final statement on Villa Grazia ('it's a very… very well known area') hint to the aura and extent of Bontate's criminal stature. The allusive code and the — again — grotesque oscillation between conflicting registers and semantic fields are key to Maresco's *Belluscone,* whose characters speak a fuzzy and ambiguous language showing their inability to establish a clear ethic relationship with the world that surrounds them. As a journalist, Maniaci should be able to use a more plain, denotative speech, but apparently he, too, is caught in the linguistic trap that entangles all the Sicilian characters of *Belluscone,* including Dell'Utri, whose *omertà* is stigmatized by means of an apparently accidental technical problem.

Quoting Sciascia, writer Giorgio Vasta argues that *Belluscone* emphasizes how this linguistic 'viscosity' has expanded to all the social classes in Palermo (2014). In fact, as Vasta shows, the processes of 'elusività' (elusion), 'reticenza' (reticence) and 'risignificazione' (re-signification) that mark the language of *Belluscone*'s lumpenproletariat also define the self-awareness, shame and oblivion in the educated and bourgeois (Ibid.). The title itself, *Belluscone. Una storia siciliana,* captures this linguistic drift, connecting it with the society that has produced it, which, in Maresco's view, is hostage of the contemporary mediatized political processes and is not only incapable of subversive or independent expression, but is also guilty of passively incorporating the mediated political discourse into archaic attitudes of *omertà* and passive submission to power. Maresco embraces this process of re-signification, creating a choral and at the same time 'aphasic'

(Vasta) and grotesque epic on *Il Cavaliere*. In the Palermo neigh-borhoods controlled by local Mafia clans (Villa Grazia, Brancac-cio), Berlusconi is only understood in the context of the Mafia, therefore, his deeds are paradoxically decontextualized and de-tached in a grotesque 'absolute epic distance' (Bakhtin 1981: 13), and become, ironically, the *gesta*.

The film's ending reinforces the overall sense of failure. On his way back to Milan, Tatti comments on Maresco's definitive 'shipwreck' (*Belluscone*) and suggests that the director title his film 'Il colpo di grazia' (The Finishing Blow) as a final admission of his self-defeat. In fact, after the arrest of Ciccio Mira in summer 2013 with charges of association with the Mafia, Maresco must abandon his idea to navigate Berlusconi's *storia siciliana* through his mafioso double. Sanguineti's comment is followed by a sur-real montage that juxtaposes a tracking shot of *neomelodico* singer Erik paying tribute to the grave of Mafia boss Stefano Bontate, with clips showing Prime Minister Matteo Renzi in Berlusconi's Mediaset TV show *Amici* (Friends) and activist and comic Beppe Grillo performing a political speech. Finally, during the cred-its, additional interviews are shown with regard to the so-called 'State-Mafia pact'.[2] The interviewees, mostly young middle-class people partying in a disco, are either unaware or unwilling to talk about this topic and strongly resist the questions. The inter-viewer's voice is not Maresco's anymore, emphasizing the disap-pearance of the director's cumbersome body and intellectual role. Maresco's absence implies that a director who wants to make a film like *Belluscone* cannot but disappear from the cinematic scene. The conventional categories used in the panorama of Ital-ian filmmaking are not valid for Maresco anymore: he is simply a 'reietto' (rejected), who is refused even by the proletariat, that is, the political body 'by which, he believes, he is loved very much',

---

2   The 'State-Mafia pact' consisted of the supposed attempt to reach an agreement between the Corleone families and the Italian government in 1992-93. Allegedly, the agreement was conceived after Cosa Nostra's strategic massacres and bombings against magistrates, politicians, and public buildings. Recently, former President of Italy, Sergio Napolitano, and other politicians were called to testify in court about the pact. Allegedly, in those years Berlusconi received funds from the Mafia. For more details, see Maurizio Torrealta (2010).

as Sanguineti explains (*Belluscone*). Commenting on the debacle
of Maresco's 'hard and pure cinema' (Ibid.) and the inevitable
depression that it lead him to, Sanguineti confirms that the con-
tamination of low and high in Maresco's cinema neither engen-
ders a liberatory carnivalesque laughter, as Bakhtin would put it
(1984), nor is the bearer of a revolutionary charge. It is a cinema
that simply cannot exist.

The Movie Selfie, *or Status Update:* Arance e martello.

Arance e martello (2014) is the first feature by blogger, journalist,
and comic Diego Bianchi, aka 'Zoro'. Openly inspired by Spike
Lee's *Do the Right Thing* and Bianchi's series of ten-minute comic
reportages known as *Tolleranza Zoro* (Zoro Tolerance), *Arance* is a
hybrid film between a comedy and a mockumentary on the dis-
array of the left- and right-wing political groups in the time of
Berlusconi. From a comic and nostalgic perspective, *Arance* dramatizes both the identity crisis of the Italian left and the radical-
ization of its conflict with conservative and neofascist groups in
Rome, and by extension, in Italy. The film is contained within the
political, social, and ethnic micro-universe of Via Orvieto in *Quartiere San Giovanni* in Rome — where the director grew up and still
lives — in summer 2011. This is the last summer of Berlusconi as
a prime minister and, as it is ironically underlined in the film, the
hottest summer in 150 years. The title *Arance e martello* (Oranges
and Hammer) is an ironic pun. It evokes the sickle ('falce') and
hammer of the communist symbol, the fresh products sold at the
San Giovanni local market, and the color palette of the film. Notwithstanding its light comic touch, *Arance* makes a powerful statement on Berlusconi by means of its metacinematic allusions and
its construction as a (fake) participatory documentary, where the
rules are in flux and new forms of political activism may develop
because of a 'participatory notion of spectatorship' (Marks 2000:
146). In fact, the film is presented in its making, with the director
and both his viewers and his subjects involved in the action and in
its political commentary. Bianchi proposes a new satirical political narrative while also putting his own persona on center stage
according to the modalities of the 'selfie' picture, which estab-

lish processes of self-reflexivity and create social circles between the filmed subjects and the viewers. In other words, by creating a 'movie selfie' (Wilson 2014: 63-76) directed to a 'digitally enhanced audience' (Ellis 2012: 45), *Arance* brings to the fore the networked contemporary culture, underscoring the 'death' of both territorial political practices and televisual models of 'centralized experience' (Jenkins, Ford, and Green, 2013: 6).

Interestingly, Maresco's and Bianchi's films take divergent paths on the question of the relationship between cinema, mediated realities, and post-ideological society. While *Belluscone* draws attention on the catastrophe of cinema, culture, and politics caused by the 'inundation' of 'digital trash',[3] *Arance* positions itself on the opposite hand of the spectrum: in an ironic but concrete way, it sanctions the decline of Berlusconi at the intersection of new digital media with politics and popular culture.

Before discussing the intricacies of the *movie selfie*, let me briefly describe the film's essential narrative. The action unfolds in one day and opens with a non-diegetic black woman's dance clearly reminiscent of the opening sequence of *Do the Right Thing*. Following the structure of Lee's film, the scene cuts to a close up of dj Malcom X, who is giving the morning weather forecast and urging people to 'wake up' (in English, quoting Señor Love Daddy) from the local radio 'Carbonara Sushi Station'. The camera then tilts up to the window for an establishing shot that introduces the viewer to the San Giovanni market. The action soon moves inside the market, which is crowded with retailers, buyers, old local residents, activists of the Democratic Party, and director Diego Bianchi, who is playing himself in the movie. In the market, he is shopping while trying to conduct interviews. The left-wing activists are a mix of peaceful people of various ages and political motivations, and are led by a harmless family of three. They are campaigning to collect 'ten million signatures' to force Silvio Berlusconi to resign (*Arance*). On the contrary, the market retailers are firm right-wing supporters, and tension arises between the two groups. The community is thrown into confusion by the news that the municipality will close the market to build a parking lot. When left-wing activists fail to take concrete political action to

---

3   See this book, p. 88.

support the retailers against this resolution, the market people occupy the Democratic Party's headquarters. Regardless of the arrival of the city mayor and the media circus that surrounds him, the occupation goes ahead and turns into a catastrophe: a fire develops and one of the retailers is shot with a rifle owned by a former partisan. Bianchi has been filming the progression of events for the whole day and he hopes that this will be the film of his life, but eventually a fireman spraying a water hose to put out fire damages his camera. The film ends with Bianchi crying at the entrance of the party's premises while dj Malcom X is commenting on the disaster and urging the listeners to *wake up.*

The choral dimension and 'territorial inscription' of *Do the Right Thing* (Pouzoulet 1997: 33) blend smoothly with the comic political drama of the community of *Arance.* However, the most original trait of *Arance* is the self-inscription of the filmmaker within the narration, which takes place at many levels. On one hand, Bianchi fully participates in the action, acting as a mediator and an impromptu leader in the petty political debates taking place throughout the film — both within the Democratic Party and between the left- and the right-wing groups. He is a sort of Mookie in Roman dialect, and the insistence on his metacinematic role as a filmmaker also hints to Lee. On the other hand,

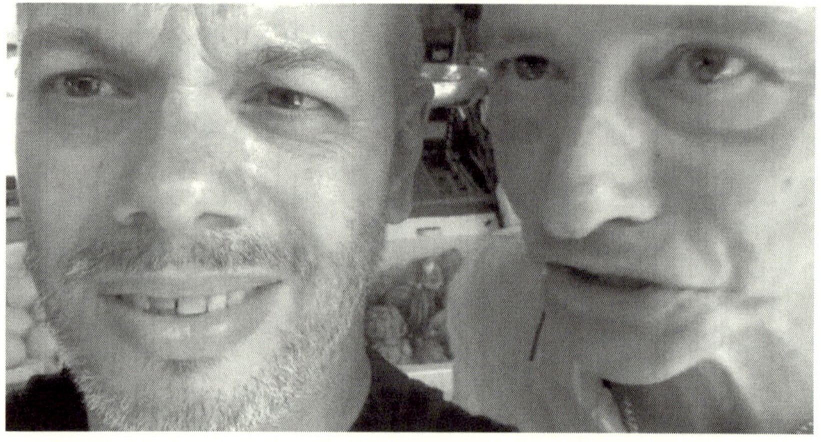

Figure 33. Bianchi in the mode, while interviewing the greengrocer of the market.

Bianchi often switches to the *movie selfie* mode, turning his camera on himself. The *movie selfie* in *Arance* follows two main modalities. The first one establishes a private space for the filmmaker to interview one or more subjects on film. The second one offers a subjective point of view on a scene taking place behind the filmmaker himself, that he controls from his camera flip screen. To emphasize the difference between regular filmmaking and *movie selfie*, the color palette also changes, respectively, from the dominant orange to more natural and cool tones. In figures 33 and 34 Bianchi is filming the *movie selfie* in the first mode while interviewing, respectively, a greengrocer and two women who sell fish at the market. In these interactions, Bianchi and the subjects fill the frame and tend to look at themselves or in the camera, as it is typical of the 'selfie' modality. The technique has multifold effects. It creates a sense of familiarity and intimacy between director and characters while estranging them from the film action and establishing a communication path with a virtual audience. It also emphasizes Bianchi's self-reflexive position and autobiographical role within the narrative. Selfie-filming is a relatively new phenomenon and there are only a few studies on the topic (mainly on selfie still pictures); however, Gavin Wilson's work on the *movie selfie* made with cellphones has shed light on interest-

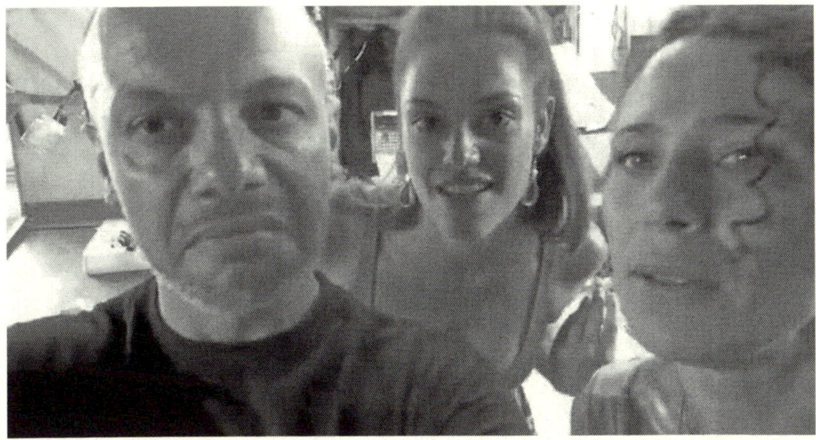

Figure 34. Bianchi in the *movie selfie* mode, interviewing two women who sell fish at the market.

ing concepts that seem fully at work in *Arance*. Wilson argues that selfie-filming endows a movie with 'the directness of address of documentary film whilst maintaining a subjective treatment of events.' (2014: 77). Because of *movie selfies'* characteristic duality, which involves 'the filmmaker directing their gaze directly to camera, they become remembered accounts of personal expressions of lives being lived, *movie selfies* that also signify other narrative complexities' (Ibid. Emphasis is in the text). Wilson emphasizes that the relative absence of professional paraphernalia turns the *movie selfie* into a 'personalized enunciation' that avoids fictionalizing strategies, promotes 'inter-personal immediacy', and removes 'a complicating additional layer of mediation.' (Ibid.) In other words, the *movie selfie* conveys an impression of authenticity and a feeling of persuasiveness that is difficult to achieve in more orthodox documentaries.

The other modality of the *movie selfie*, that is, the self-inscription of the director's face with a scene behind him (figure 35), is even more meaningful. This mode drastically reverses the principle of cinema *vérité*, insofar as it makes the viewer constantly aware of the camera, and it also frames Bianchi in an apparent position of power within the scene. He deliberately uses facial expressions to ironically comment on what is happening, thus establishing a comic communication mode with the (virtual) viewers. Again,

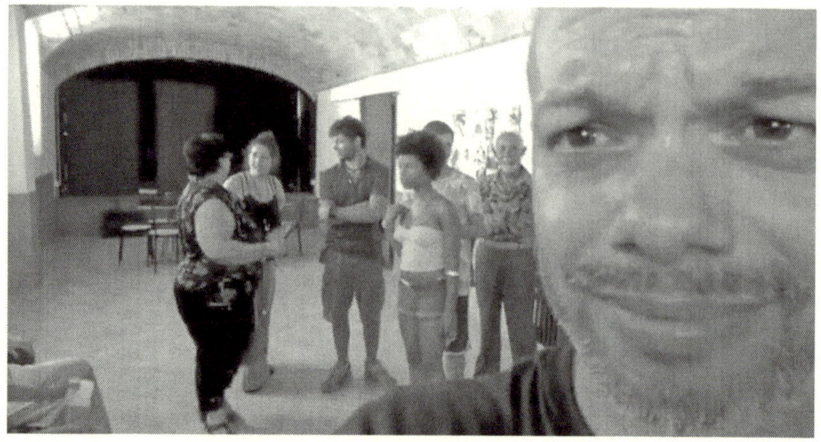

Figure 35. Bianchi making a *movie selfie* with people behind him.

the pervasive presence of the director's persona and the alternation between *movie selfie*, subjective, and objective camera endow the accidental events of the *quartiere* with an increasing sense of authenticity and a self-contained narrative status (Dalla Gassa 2014: 336).

Bianchi's apparent position of privilege and power, however, is only illusory. His entitlement as a director, both of the film and of the ongoing conflict, is ironically deconstructed in the long double dolly shot that interrupts the occupation evoking the race rant of *Do the Right Thing* (figure 36). This time, Bianchi's frontal position and look into the camera are not part of the cinematography of the *movie selfie*. This is in fact a non-diegetic shot that allows Bianchi to vent his frustration and sense of inadequacy as a nostalgic left-wing activist turned into the inept director of a futile socio-political documentary. His monologue is illuminating:

> I wanted to make the documentary on the market, then the documentary on the discussion in the party, then the documentary on the occupation. Now I can do everything: film, DVD, book, actor, director, screenwriter, musician. I can do anything, I can. I don't know how to do anything. I'm cool because I don't know how to do anything. I know it, they don't know it. I'm cool because I'm left-winger, nostalgic. I'm the gut of the militant even though I haven't been active in twenty years. I'm a radical chic, snobbish, an

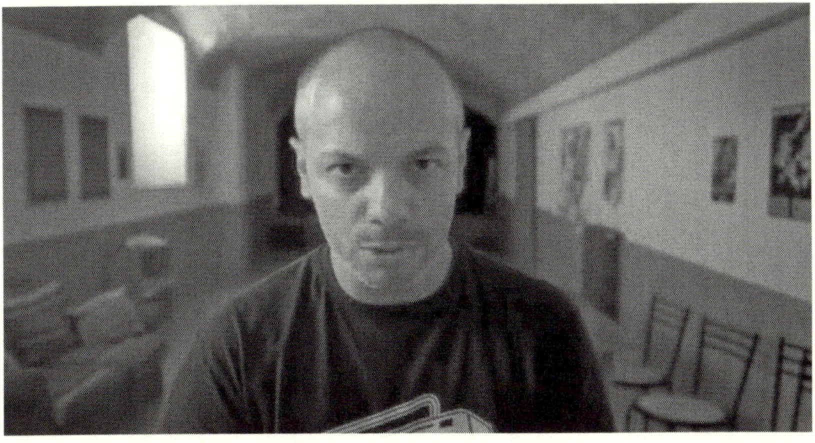

Figure 36. Bianchi in the rant scene.

armchair leftist, I'm a friend of everybody who's pissed me off. I'm the same as those who pissed me off. I make them laugh and think, think and cry, I make you cry. (*Arance*)

As the race rant of the characters looking in the camera in *Do the Right Thing* is meant to solicit the reaction of the viewers according to a sort of Brechtian strategy of estrangement (Kellner 1997: 74-78), the self-deprecating rant of *Arance* — which involves the other characters as well — is an attempt to *wake up* the failed left-wing activists who have become incapable of any meaningful political action. In a collective and generational *movie selfie*, Bianchi turns his camera toward the 'armchair leftists' who waste their time to collect 'ten million signatures' to force Berlusconi to resign, while his caricatural subjects shoot at each other as they would do at the time of the Resistance.

Interestingly, the self-referential digital universe documented in the *movie selfies* of *Arance* parallels the grotesque analog microcosmos of the Sicilian landscape of *Belluscone*. In both films, Berlusconi is the trigger of the two directors' crisis and the grotesque reflection of their own political and ethical concerns.

6.
EPILOGUE

Despite his ubiquitous presence in Italian limelight for more than two decades, Berlusconi's public history is coming to an end. Nonetheless, interest in his persona's 'semiotic excess' (Fiske 1986: 403) continues to flourish. This analysis has attempted to uncover his multifold representations in cinema across modes and time, from narrative to non-fiction films, from the proto-Berlusconi of Comedy Italian Style to Maresco's and Bianchi's tragicomic self-reflections. This exploration — albeit not exhaustive — has shown how Berlusconi's body is a polysemic cultural construct, whose interpretation changes based on the interests, aspirations, and desires of the filmmakers and the viewers.

In the corpus of the narrative films discussed in this book, these interpretations take shape in a variety of ways: connections to pre-existing ideas of 'national character' (*La più bella giornata*), confrontations with ethical and aesthetic challenges posed by neotelevision (*Ginger e Fred*), deconstructions of mediated appearances of power (*La bella addormentata*), awareness of the conflicting relationship between public and personal spheres (*Viva la libertà*), evocations of Italian historical specters, such as Aldo Moro (*Bye Bye*), encounters with overwhelming existential and social issues (*Belluscone*), the scapegoating of political enemies (*Shooting Silvio*), and the challenging reassessment of political constituencies (*Arance*).

The non-fictional films present a similar variety of interpretations. The documentaries analyzed in this book pinpoint Berlusconi's ascent to power and his progressive spectralization and removal. There are several significant documentaries about Berlusconi that are not discussed in this volume. Space limitation forced me to make choices. The documentaries presented were chosen because they all center on Berlusconi's political career and, as a group, they illustrate his parable in a powerful way. On the other hand, those not included focus on particular themes and a discussion of them in this book would have required much more space. But they are captivating stories. For example, Sabina Guzzanti's *Viva Zapatero!* (2005) follows Guzzanti's struggle against media censorship after her controversial television program, *RAIot*, was banned by public TV channels. In *La trattativa* (The State-Mafia Pact, 2014), Guzzanti explores the notorious pact between political institutions and the Mafia. Gandini's *Videocracy* (2009) goes back to the historical roots of Berlusconi's networks and denounces the hypersexualization of the female body, typical of his television broadcasts. Gnetti and Fracassi's *Le dame e il Cavaliere* (The Dames and The Knight, 2010) centers on the *bunga bunga* season and the sexual scandals with Noemi Letizia, Patrizia D'Addario, and other young women. In *Sorelle d'Italia* (Sisters of Italy, 2010), Robbiani and Buccella travel throughout Italy to interview women of different ages and backgrounds about Berlusconi. Finally, Annalisa Pira's *Girlfriend in a Coma* is a caustic exploration of 'mala' (bad) and 'buona' (good) Italy through social and demographic data, landscapes, people, and politicians.

An analysis of Berlusconi in cinema is an ongoing process. I am hopeful that this volume will inspire viewers and scholars to watch and discuss its corpus and beyond. For example, one project currently in pre-production is Roberta Torre's satirical musical *La caduta dell'impero* (The Collapse of the Empire), a 'dramaturgic reflection' (Torre 2013) on an ageing, declining Berlusconi who is consumed by his desire for young female bodies. *La caduta* intends to shed light on issues of gender, sexuality, and power in *Berlusconismo*. It is unlikely that Torre's will be the last film on Berlusconi, but the carnivalesque — and bestial — images of decadence in *La caduta* would be most appropriate to place the word *fine* on *Berlusconismo*.

APPENDIX

Silvio Berlusconi's Political Trajectory: A Brief Summary

Silvio Berlusconi first entered the political arena in January 1994, when he founded the new conservative party *Forza Italia*, FI (Go Italy). On 26 January 1994, he addressed the nation with the notorious talk of the *discesa in campo* (descent into the field) that he broadcasted from his TV networks. In the national elections in March 1994, the coalition led by *Forza Italia* won the majority in Parliament and Berlusconi was nominated Prime Minister for the first time. He was Prime Minister again in 2001-2006 and 2008-2011. The fusion of *Forza Italia* with the other right-wing parties of the coalition resulted in the foundation of *Popolo della Libertà*, PDL (People of Freedom) in 2008. Between 2009 and 2010, Gianfranco Fini, former leader of *Alleanza Nazionale*, AN (National Alliance) and Berlusconi's primary associate in PDL, contested Berlusconi's leadership and founded an independent association that marked his distance from PDL. The internal collapse of PDL, the international economic crisis, and Berlusconi's trials for corruption, fraud, and sex offenses led to a vote of no confidence against his government in October 2011. Berlusconi resigned on 12 November 2011. In 2013, a court's verdict sentenced him to four years in jail and banned him from holding public office until 2019. The verdict was commuted to one year and, finally, to performing social work once a week in a community for the elderly in Cesano Boscone (Milan) because at the time of the sentence Silvio Berlusconi was too old to go to jail under the Italian law. In January 2013, after strong tensions among internal factions and with the affirmation of two new leaders in the political arena, Matteo Renzi of the *Partito Democratico*, PD (Democratic Party) and Beppe Grillo of the *Movimento 5 Stelle*, M5S (5 Star Movement), Berlusconi recreated *Forza Italia*, of which, at this writing, he is still the leader.

Filmography

1. The Corpus of Films on Silvio Berlusconi

1972 *La più bella serata della mia vita*. Ettore Scola. De Laurentis/Columbia. Italy.

1985 *Ginger e Fred*. Federico Fellini. P.E.A. Italy/France/West Germany.

1996 *Fantozzi. Il ritorno*. Neri Parenti. Cecchi Gori/Italian International. Italy.

1997 *Hammamet Village*. Ninì Grassia. Produzioni Associate. Italy.

2001 *Il più migliore al mondo*. Aurelio Grimaldi. Gruppo Pasquino. Italy.

2003 *Citizen Berlusconi*. Andrea Cairola, Susan Gray. Stefilm/WNET. USA/Italy/Germany/Finland.

2003 *Sua Maestà Silvio Berlusconi*. Stéphane Bentura. Capa Presse TV Paris. France.

2004 *Dopo mezzanotte*. Davide Ferrario. Rossofuoco. Italy.

2004 *Lilli e il cavaliere*. Caterina Borelli. Anonymous Productions. Italy.

2004 *La brutta copia*. Massimo Ceccherini. Cecchi Gori. Italy.

2004 *Ladri di barzellette*. Bruno Colella, Leonardo Giuliano. Italgest/Le Grand Bleu. Italy.

2005 *Bye Bye Berlusconi*. Jan Henrik Stahlberg. Schiwago Film. Germany.

2005 *Quando c'era Silvio*. Beppe Cremagnani, Enrico Deaglio. Luben. Italy.

2005 *Grazie Berlusconi!* Fulvia Alberti. Article Z. France.

2005 *Viva Zapatero!* Sabina Guzzanti. Lucky Red/Sciocco. Italy.

2006 *Berlusconi, Affaire Mondadori*. Mosco Boucault. ARTE Francia/Zex. France.

2006 *Il Caimano*. Nanni Moretti. Sacher/Bac/Stephan/France 3. Italy/France.

2006 *In un altro paese*. Marco Turco. Doclab/Artline Films/RAI 3/France 2.

2007 *Shooting Silvio*. Berardo Carboni. Mork e Berry/Kubla Khan. Italy.

2007 *Ops... Ho ammazzato Berlusconi!*. Gianluca Rossi, Daniele Giometto. Collepardo Film. Italy.

2009 *Videocracy. Basta apparire*. Erik Gandini. Atmo AB/Zentropa. Sweden.

2010 *Draquila. L'Italia che trema*. Sabina Guzzanti. Sciocco. Italy.

2010 *Le dame e il cavaliere*. Francesca Gnetti, Franco Fracassi. Telemaco. Italy.

2010 *Sorelle d'Italia*. Lorenzo Buccella, Vito Robbiani. mediaTREE/Amka. Switzerland

2011 *Silvio Forever.* Roberto Faenza and Filippo Macelloni. Ad Hoc Film. Italy.
2011 *Italy: Love It or Leave It.* Gustav Hofer, Luca Ragazzi. hiq/NDR/WDR/RAITre. Italy.
2012 *La bella addormentata.* Marco Bellocchio. Cattleya. Italy.
2012 *S.B. Io lo conoscevo bene.* Giacomo Durzi, Giovanni Fasanella. Kinesis. Italy.
2012 *Girlfriend in a Coma.* Bill Emmot and Annalisa Pira. Springshot. U.K.
2013 *Viva la libertà.* Roberto Andò. Bibi Film TV. Italy.
2014 *Belluscone. Una storia siciliana.* Franco Maresco. Rean Mazzone, Zen Zero. Italy.
2014 *Arance e martello.* Diego Bianchi. Fandango. Italy.
2014 *La trattativa.* Sabina Guzzanti. Secol Superbo e Sciocco. Italy.
(Pre-production) *La caduta dell'impero.* Roberta Torre.

2. Other Films Cited

8½, dir. Federico Fellini, 1963
Apocalypse now, dir. Francis Ford Coppola, 1979
L'arte di arrangiarsi (The art of Figuring It Out), dir. Luigi Zampa, 1954
Buongiorno, notte (*Good Morning, Night*), dir. Marco Bellocchio, 2003
Che, dir. Steven Soderbergh, 2008
The Deal, dir. Stephen Frears, 2003
Death of a President, dir. Gabriel Range, 2007
Downfall, dir. Oliver Hirschbiegel, 2004
Il divo: La spettacolare vita di Giulio Andreotti (Il Divo: The Spectacular Life of Giulio Andreotti), dir. Paolo Sorrentino, 2008
La dolce vita, dir. Federico Fellini, 1960
Enzo, domani a Palermo! (Enzo, Tomorrow in Palermo!), dir. Daniele Ciprì, Franco Maresco, 1999
Frost/Nixon, dir. Ron Howard, 2008
Gandhi, dir. Richard Attenborough, 1982
The Interview, dir. Seth Rogen and Evan Goldberg, 2014
Io sono Tony Scott (I Am Tony Scott), dir. Antonio Maresco, 2010
The Iron Lady, dir. Phyllida Lloyd, 2011
JFK, dir. Oliver Stone, 1991
The Last King of Scotland, dir. Kevin Macdonald, 2006
Lincoln, dir. Steven Spielberg, 2012
Il medico della mutua (The Primary Care Physician), dir. Luigi Zampa, 1968
Il moralista (The Moralist), dir. Giorgio Bianchi, 1959
Morgan: A Suitable Case for Treatment, dir. Karel Reisz, 1966
Noi credevamo (We Believed), dir. Mario Martone, 2010

Rumble Fish, dir. Francis Ford Coppola 1983
Lo sceicco bianco (*The White Sheik*), dir. Federico Fellini, 1952
Selma, dir. Ava DuVernay, 2014
Team America: World Police, dir. Trey Parker, 2004
The Queen, dir. Stephen Frears, 2006
Il ritorno di Cagliostro (The Return of Cagliostro), dir. Franco Maresco, Dan-
    iele Ciprì, 2003
The Special Relationship, dir. Richiard Loncraine, 2010
Il vigile (The Street Policeman), dir. Luigi Zampa, 1960
Vincere (Win), dir. Marco Bellocchio, 2009
I vitelloni, dir. Federico Fellini, 1953
W., dir. Olver Stone, 2008

BIBLIOGRAPHY

Abruzzese, A. and V. Susca (eds). 2004. *Tutto è Berlusconi: radici, metafore e destinazione del tempo nuovo* (Milan: Lupetti)

Agamben, Giorgio. 2011. *The Kingdom and the Glory*, trans. by L. Chiesa (Stanford: Stanford University Press)

Agnew, A. John. 2011. 'The Big Seducer: Berlusconi's Image at Home and Abroad and the Future of Italian Politics', *California Italian Studies* 2, 1, Web http://escholarship.org/uc/item/2bt6w92c [Accessed 28 December 2012]

Albertazzi D, C. Brook, C. Ross, and N. Rothenbergh (eds). 2009. *Resisting the Tide. Cultures of Opposition Under Berlusconi (2001-06)* (New York-London: Continuum)

Anderson, Perry. 2002. 'Land without Prejudice', *London Review of Books*, 6, 21 March, Web. http://www.lrb.co.uk/v24/n06/perry-anderson/land-without-prejudice [accessed 2 August 2014]

Andò, Roberto. 2012. *Il trono vuoto* (Milan: Bompiani)

Anon. 2013.'Emmott contro Maxxi e Ministero della Cultura. "Girlfriend in a coma" rinviata per le elezioni', in *La Repubblica*, 1 February http://www.repubblica.it/politica/2013/02/01/news/emmott_su_twitter_cancellati_da_maxxi-51728869/ [Accessed 12 November 2014]

—. 2009. 'Sky manda in onda "Shooting Silvio". PDL all'attacco della TV di Murdoch', in *La Repubblica,* April 14 http://www.repubblica.it/2009/04/sezioni/politica/shooting-silvio/shooting-silvio/shooting-silvio.html [Accessed 12 November 12 2014].

Antonello, Pierpaolo. 2013. 'I due corpi del divo: le maschere del potere: Andreotti, Thatcher, Elisabetta II', *Bianco e Nero*, 2-3: 160-67

—. 2012a. 'Di crisi in meglio. realismo, impegno postmoderno e cinema politico nell'Italia degli anni zero: da Nanni Moretti a Paolo Sorrentino', *Italian Studies*, 67, 2, July: 169–87

—. 2012b. 'Un impegno "postmoderno"', in Vito Zagarrio (ed.), *Nanni Moretti. Lo sguardo morale* (Venice-Pesaro: Marsilio), pp. 47-52

Antonello, P. and F. Mussgung (eds). 2009. *Postmodern Impegno. Ethics and Commitment in Contemporary Italian Culture* (Oxford: Peter Lang)

Bakhtin, Mikhail M. 1984. *Rabelais and His World*, trans. by H. Iswolsky (Bloomington: Indiana University Press)

—. 1981. 'Epic and Novel', in Michael Holquist (ed.), *The dialogic Imagination* (Austin: University of Texas Press, 1981), pp. 3-40

Banfield, Edward. 1958. *The Moral Basis of a Backward Society* (Glencoe, Illinois: The Free Press)

Baransky Z., and R. Lumley (eds). 1990. *Culture and Conflict in Post War Italy: Essays on Mass and Popular Culture* (New York: St. Martin's Press)

Barra, L. and M. Scaglioni. 2013. 'Berlusconi's Television, Before and After. The 1980s, innovation and conservation', *Comunicazioni sociali*, 1: 79-89

Barthes, Roland. 1975. *The Pleasure of the Text*, trans. by R. Miller (New York: Hill and Wang)

Baty S., Paige. 1995. *American Monroe: The Making of a Body Politic* (Berkeley: University of California Press)

Belpoliti, Marco. 2009. *Il corpo del capo* (Parma: Guanda)

Berlusconi, Silvio. 1994. 'La discesa in campo di Silvio Berlusconi'. *Corriere della Sera*, 26 January http://video.corriere.it/discesa-campo-silvio-berlusconi/5040d3d4-0d59-11e1-a42a-1562b6741916 [accessed July 24 2014]

Berlusconi, Veronica. 2007. 'Veronica Berlusconi, lettera a Repubblica. "Mio marito mi deve pubbliche scuse"' *Repubblica*, 31 January http://www.repubblica.it/2007/01/sezioni/politica/lettera-veronica/lettera-veronica/lettera-veronica.html [accessed July 24 2014]

'Berlusconismo e Fascismo' (1). 2011. *Micromega 1*

'Berlusconismo e Fascismo' (2). 2011. *Micromega 2*

Bobbio, Norberto. 2008. *Contro i nuovi dispotismi. Scritti sul* berlusconismo (Bari: Dedalo)

Bolton, L. and C. Siggers Manson (eds). 2007. *Italy on Screen: National Identity and Italian Imaginary* (London: IGRS)

Bondanella, Peter. 2009 '*Commedia all'Italiana*', in *A History of Italian Cinema* (London-New York: Bloomsbury), pp. 180-216

—. 2002. *The Films of Federico Fellini* (Cambridge: Cambridge University Press)

Bonsaver, Guido. 2007. 'The Caiman', *Sight and Sound*, May, p. 56

Bradshaw, Peter. 2006. 'The Caiman', *The Guardian*, 23 May http://www.theguardian.com/film/2006/may/23/cannes2006.cannesfilmfestival1 [Accessed 2 February 2012]

Brook, Clodagh. 2009. 'The Cinema of Resistance: Nanni Moretti's *Il caimano* and the Italian Film Industry', in Albertazzi D., C. Brook, C. Ross, and N. Rothenbergh (eds), *Resisting the Tide. Cultures of Opposition Under Berlusconi (2001-06)* (New York-London: Continuum), pp. 11-23

Brown, T., and B. Vidal. 2014. *The Biopic in Contemporary Film Culture* (New York: Routledge)

Bruni, Frank. 2013. 'The Mummy Returns', *New York Times*, 22 February http://www.nytimes.com/2013/02/24/opinion/sunday/bruni-berlusconi-is-back.html?pagewanted=2&_r=0&ref=frankbruni [Accessed July 20 2014]

Carlorosi, Silvia. 2012. 'Politica cinema e società nel *Caimano* di Moretti', *NEMLA Italian Studies*, XXXIV: 87-108

Casetti, Francesco. 1998. *Inside the Gaze. The Fiction Film and Its Spectator* (Bloomington: Indiana University Press)

Castelli, Valeria. 2001. 'Is *Citizen Berlusconi* good for democracy? A "global documentary" about Italy's anomalies', *Studies in Documentary Film*, V, 2-3: 223-234

Ceccarelli, Filippo. 2006. 'Moretti e il berlusconismo è il giorno del Caimano' *La Repubblica*, 23 May [Accessed 24 August 2014]

Ceccarelli, Leah. 1998. 'Polysemy: Multiple Meanings in Rhetorical Criticism,' *Quarterly Journal of Speech*, 84, 4, 394-414.

Chiaramonte, A., and R. D'Alimonte. 2012. 'The Twilight of the Berlusconi Era: Local Elections and National Referendums in Italy, May and June 2011', *South European Society and Politics*, 17, 2: 261-279

Comand, Mariapia. 2010. *Commedia all'italiana* (Milan: Il Castoro)

Condit, Celeste. 1991. 'The Rhetorical Limits of Polysemy', in R. K. Avery and D. Eason (eds), *Critical Perspectives on Media and Society* (New York: Methuen),

Cordero, Franco. 2002. 'Il signore della propaganda e un paese senza passioni', *La Repubblica* 15 May, p. 15

Dalla Gassa, Marco. 2014. 'Selfie-control. Il dispositivo che fotografa se stesso', *Fata Morgana*, VIII, 2: 329-38

Dargis, M. and A.O. Scott. 2012. 'The Cannes Festival: News makes "*Caiman*" all but history', *The New York Times*, 23 May http://www.nytimes.com/2006/05/23/arts/23iht-notebook24.html?_r=0   [Accessed 2 February 2012]

Debord, Guy. 1967. *La Sociéte du Spectacle* (Paris: Gallimard; third ed. 1992)

Deaglio, Enrico. 2014. *Indagine sul ventennio* (Milan: Feltrinelli)

Dei, Fabio. 2011. 'Pop-politica: le basi culturali del berlusconismo', *Studi Culturali* VII, 3, December: 471-89.

De Gaetano, Roberto. 2012. *Nanni Moretti. Lo smarrimento del presente* (Cosenza: Luigi Pellegrini Editore) Kindle ebook

——. 2009. 'Rappresentare il presente. *Il caimano* di Moretti e la commedia grottesca, in R. Guerrini, G. Tagliani, F. Zucconi (eds), *Lo spazio del reale nel cinema italiano contemporaneo* (Genova: Le Mani), pp. 51-59

——.1999. *Il corpo e la maschera. Il grottesco nel cinema italiano* (Rome: Bulzoni)

Dominijanni, Ida. 2014a. *Il trucco* (Rome: Ediesse)

——. 2014b. 'The Cricket's Leap. Post-Oedipal Populism and Neoliberal Democracy in Contemporary Italy'. *Cultural Critique* 87, Spring: 167-82

Dürrenmatt, Friedrich. *Traps*, trans. by R. and C. Winston (New York: Knopf)

Eco, Umberto. 1983. 'TV: la trasparenza perduta', *Sette anni di desiderio* (Milan: Bompiani), pp. 163-79

Ellis, John. 2012. *Documentary: Witness and Self-revelation* (New York: Routledge)

Eyerman, Ron. 2011. *The Cultural Sociology of Political Assassination: From MLK and RFK to Fortyn and van Gogh* (New York: Palgrave)

Falci, Giuseppe Alberto. 2014. 'B. assolto, le tentazioni di Forza Italia: ritorno al governo e alleanza con Ncd'. *Il Fatto Quotidiano*, 20 July http://www.ilfattoquotidiano.it/2014/07/20/b-assolto-le-tentazioni-di-forza-italia-ritorno-al-governo-e-alleanza-con-ncd/1066620/ [Accessed 23 July 2014]

Fini, Gianfranco. 2013. *Il Ventennio. Io, Berlusconi e la destra tradita* (Milan: Rizzoli)

Fiori, Giuseppe. 1995. *Il venditore. Storia di Silvio Berlusconi e della Fininvest* (Milan: Garzanti)

Fish, Stanley E. 1982. *Is There a Text in This Class? The Authority of Interpretive Communities* (Cambridge, MA: Harvard University Press)

Fiske, John. 1986. 'Television: Polysemy and Popularity', *Critical Studies in Mass Communication*, 3: 391-405

Fofi, Goffredo. 2004. *Alberto Sordi. L'Italia in bianco e nero* (Milan: Mondadori)

Forza Italia. 2001. *Una storia italiana* (Milan: Mondadori)

Foucault, Michel.1984. 'Preface to The History of Sexuality, Volume II', in *The Foucault Reader*. Ed. by Paul Rabinow (New York: Pantheon Books), pp. 333-9.

—.1978. *The History of Sexuality, Volume I: An Introduction*. Trans. Robert Hurley (New York: Penguin Books)

Galli della Loggia, Ernesto. 1998. *L'identità nazionale* (Bologna: Il Mulino)

Gargiulo, Gius. 2010. 'Baroque néo-mélodique et barock'n'roll. Les identités musicales à Naples dans les années 1970', *Les Cahiers du MIM-MOC* [En ligne], 6 http://mimmoc.revues.org/519 [Accessed 3 October 2015]

Genovese, Rino. 2011. *Che cos'è il Berlusconismo* (Rome: Manifestolibri)

Gerbner, George. 1998. 'Cultivation Analysis: an Overview', *Mass Communication and Society*, 1, 3/4: 175-94

Ghezzi, Enrico. 2014. 'Verifica incerta', *Blob*, RAI 3, 2 September 2014

Gibelli, Antonio. 2010. *Berlusconi passato alla storia. L'Italia nell'era della democrazia autoritaria* (Rome: Donzelli)

Giannini, Massimo. 2008. *Lo statista. Il ventennio berlusconiano tra fascismo e populismo* (Milan: Baldini Castoldi)

Ginsborg, Paul. 2004. *Silvio Berlusconi. Television, Power, and Patrimony* (London-New York: Verso)

Ginsborg, P., and E. Asquer (eds). 2011. *Berlusconismo. Analisi di un sistema di potere* (Bari: Laterza).

Goffman, Erwin. 1959. *The Presentation of Self in Everyday Life* (New York: Doubleday)

Grande, Maurizio. 2003. *La commedia all'italiana*, ed. by Orio Caldiron (Rome: Bulzoni)

Grasso, Aldo. 2000. *Storia della televisione italiana* (Milan: Garzanti)

Guicciardini, Francesco. 1576. *Consigli et Avvertimenti* (Paris: Morel)

Gundle, Stephen. 1998. 'The death (and re-birth) or the hero: Charisma and manufactured charisma in modern Italy', *Modern Italy*, 3, 2: 173-89

—. 1995. 'Il sorriso di Berlusconi', *Altrochemestre*, 3, Summer: 14-17.

Hall, Stuart. 1980. 'Encoding/Decoding', in Hall, S., D. Hobson, A. Lowe, and P. Willis, *Culture, Media, Language; Working Papers in Cultural Studies, 1972-79* (New York: Unwin Hyman), pp. 117-27

Hartley, John. 1984. 'Encouraging Signs: Television and the Power of Dirt, Speech, and Scandalous Categories', in W. Rowland and B. Watkins, *Interpreting Television: Current Research Perspectives* (Newbury Park, CA: Sage), pp. 119-41

Hogarth, David. 2006. *Realer Than Reel: Global Directions in Documentary* (Austin, TX: University of Texas Press)

Jenkins, Henry, S. Ford, and J. Green. 2013. *Spreadable Media: Creating Value and Meaning in a Networked Culture* (New York: New York University Press)

Kantorowicz, Ernst H. 1957. *The King's Two Bodies: A Study in Mediaeval Political Theology.* (Princeton: Princeton University Press)

La Repubblica, 12 April, 2015 http://www.repubblica.it/topics/news/processo_mediaset-64029241/ [Accessed 12 April 2015]

Kellner, Douglas. 1997. 'Aesthetics, Ethics, and Politics, in the Films of Spike Lee', in Mark A. Reid (ed.), *Spike Lee's Do the Right Thing* (Cambridge: Cambridge University Press), 5-72

Lombardi, Marco. 2012. 'Volente o nolente, io "sono" anche Silvio Berlusconi', blogpost in Beppe Severgnini's 'Italians', *Corriere della Sera*, 11 December, http://italians.corriere.it/2011/11/12/volente-o-nolente-io-"sono"-anche-silvio-berlusconi [Accessed 21 July 2014]

Mancini, Paolo. 2011. *Between Commodification and Lifestyle Politics. Does Silvio Berlusconi provide a New Model of Politics for the Twenty-first Century?* (Oxford: RISJ, University of Oxford)

Manzoli, Giacomo. 2013. *Da Ercole a Fantozzi. Cinema popolare e società italiana dal boom economico alla neotelevisione* (Rome: Carocci)

Marcus, Millicent. 2002. *After Fellini* (Baltimore: The Johns Hopkins Univeristy Press)

Maresco, Franco. 2013. Unpublished interview conducted via Skype by Nicoletta Marini-Maio, 15 May

Marini-Maio, Nicoletta. 'Before and After Silvio: A Corpus for Us All', in G. Lombardi and C. Uva (eds), *Nuovo cinema politico* (Oxford: Peter Lang, forthcoming)

—. *A Specter Is Haunting Italy: The Representation of the Moro Affair in Film and Theater* (forthcoming)

Marks, Laura. 2000. *The Skin of the Film: Intercultural Cinema, Embodiment and the Senses* (Durham, NC and London: Duke University Press)

Marino, Giuseppe Carlo. 2001. *I padrini: da Vito Cascio Ferro a Lucky Luciano, da Calogero Vizzini a Stefano Bontate, fatti, segreti e testimonianze di Cosa nostra attraverso le sconcertanti biografie dei suoi protagonisti* (Rome: Newton and Compton)

Mariotti, Claudia. 2011. 'Berlusconism: Some Empirical Research'. *Bulletin of Italian Politics* 3, 1: 35-57

Masi, Stefano. 2006. *Ettore Scola. Uno sguardo acuto e ironico sull'Italia e gli italiani degli ultimi quarant'anni* (Rome: Gremese)

Menarini, Roy. 2012. 'Una galleria italiana: personaggi, ruoli mestieri', in Vito Zagarrio (ed.) *Lo sguardo morale* (Venice-Pesaro: Marsilio), pp. 104-09

Minuz, Andrea. 2014. 'Breve storia del "Degrado Morale" (e della sua trasformazione in genere cinematografico italiano)', *Nuovi argomenti*, 66, June: 187-90

—. 2013. 'Il sogno di una cosa: Un PD con Berlusconi, ovvero Viva La Libertà'
http://blog.rubbettinoeditore.it/andrea-minuz/il-sogno-di-una-cosa-un-pd-con-berlusconi-ovvero-viva-la-liberta/ [Accessed 5 March 2015]

—. 2012. *Viaggio al termine dell'Italia. Fellini politico* (Soveria Mannelli: Rubettino)

Mondini, S. and C. Semenza. 2006. 'Research Report: How Berlusconi Keeps His Face: A Neuropsychological Study in a Case of Semantic Dementia', *Cortex* 42, 3:332-35.

Nichols, Bill. 2010. *Introduction to Documentary* (Bloomington: Indiana University Press) Kindle ebook

O'Leary, Alan. 2012. 'Locations of Moro: The Kidnap in the Cinema', in G. Lombardi, R. S. Glynn (eds), *Remembering Aldo Moro: The Cultural Legacy of the 1978 Kidnapping and Murder.* (Oxford: Legenda)

—. 2011. 'Memory, Chaostory, Fiction', http://italiancinema-mumbai.tumblr.com/post/9594940204/memory-chaostory-fiction [Accessed 23 August 2014]

O'Rawe, Catherine. 2014. *Stars and Masculinities in Contemporary Italian Cinema* (New York: Palgrave)

Orsina, Giovanni. 2014. 'Due questioni sul "ritorno" di Berlusconi', *La Stampa*, 22 July http://www.lastampa.it/2014/07/22/cultura/opinioni/editoriali/due-questioni-sul-ritorno-di-berlusconi-pwnXTuHh-WuU87AkW7MKUFO/pagina.html [Accessed 22 July 2014]

—. 2013. *Il Berlusconismo nella storia d'Italia* (Venice: Marsilio) Kindle ebook

Ortoleva, Peppino. 1995. *Un ventennio a colori. Televisione privata e società in Italia (1975-95)* (Florence: Giunti)

Palaver, Wolfgang. 2013. *René Girard Mimetic Theory*, trans. by G. Borrud (East Lansing: Michigan State University Press)

Pasolini, Pier Paolo. 1999. '10 giugno 1974. Studio sulla rivoluzione antropologica in Italia', in *Scritti corsari*, in *Saggi sulla politica e sulla società*, ed. by W. Siti and S. De Laude (Milan: Mondadori), p. 309

Patriarca, Silvana. 2010. *Italianità. La costruzione del carattere nazionale.* (Rome-Bari: Laterza)

Peirce, Charles Sanders. 1998. 'Nomenclature and Divisions of Triadic Relations, as Far as They are Determined,' in The Peirce Edition Project ed.), *The Essential Peirce: Selected Philosophical Writings* (Bloomington and Indianapolis: Indiana University Press)

Perna, Vincenzo. 2014. 'Killer Melodies: The *Musica Neomelodica* Debate', in F. Fabbri and G. Plastino, *Made in Italy: Studies in Popular Musi,* (New York and London: Routledge), pp. 194-206

Povoledo, Elisabetta. 2014. 'Conviction of Berlusconi in Sex Case Is Overturned', *The New York Times,* 19 July, p. A4

Pouzoulet, Catherine. 1997. 'The Cinema of Spike Lee: Images of a Mosaic City', in Mark A. Reid (ed.), *Spike Lee's Do the Right Thing* (Cambridge: Cambridge University Press), pp. 31-49

Ricciardi, Alessia. 2012. *After La Dolce Vita: A Cultural Prehistory of Berlusconi Italy* (Stanford: Stanford University Press) Kindle ebook

Reich, Jacqueline. 2004. *Beyond the Latin Lover: Marcello Mastroianni, Masculinity, and Italian Cinema* (Bloomington: Indiana University Press)

Rigoletto, Sergio. 2007. 'The Italian Comedy of the Economic Miracle: L'*italiano medio* and Strategies of Gender Exclusion', in L. Bolton and C. Siggers Manson (ed.), *Italy on Screen: National Identity and Italian Imaginary* (London: IGRS)

Saleri, Andrea. 2003. *L'omicidio Berlusconi* (Massa: Edizioni Clandestine)

Scaglioni, Massimo. 2015. 'Television as a Project. The relation between public service broadcasting and Italian historical cultures', *Comunicazioni sociali* 1, 7-21

Sciascia, Leonardo. 1979. *La Sicilia come metafora* (Milan: Mondadori)

Santomassimo, Gianpasquale (ed.). 2005. *La notte della democrazia italiana. Dal regime fascista al governo Berlusconi* (Milan: Il Saggiatore, 2005)

Seger, Monica. 2012. 'Unattainable horizons: On history, man and land in the films of Ciprì and Maresco', *The Italianist,* 32: 256-72

Severgnini, Beppe. *La pancia degli Italiani. Berlusconi spiegato ai posteri* (Milan: Rizzoli, 2011)

Spinazzola, Vittorio. 1985. *Cinema e pubblico: Lo spettacolo filmico in Italia 1945-1965* (Rome: Bulzoni)

Squires, Nick. 2011. 'Berlusconi on Trial: Sad Story of "Ruby the Heart Stealer"', *The Telegraph,* 23 April http://www.telegraph.co.uk/news/worldnews/silvio-berlusconi/8423474/Berlusconi-on-trial-Sad-story-of-Ruby-the-Heart-Stealer.html [Accessed 23 July 2014]

Stille, Alexander. 2014. 'La voglia di essere diversi', *La Repubblica,* 23 July http://ricerca.repubblica.it/repubblica/archivio/repubblica/2014/07/23/la-voglia-di-essere-diversi29.html?ref=search [Accessed 23 July 2014]

——. 2006. *Citizen Berlusconi* (Milan: Garzanti)

St. Ours, Kathryn. 2011. 'The Time-Image from Pasolini to Ciprì and Maresco', *Romance Notes,* 51, 2: 199-208

Sutton, Paul. 2009. '"Say Something Left-Wing!" Nanni Moretti's *Il Caimano*', *Studies in European Cinema*, 6, 2-3: 141-52

Tagliani, Giacomo. 2014. 'Depicting life, analyzing the power: The "actuality" of Italian cinema', *Journal of Italian Cinema & Media Studies*, 2, 2: 199-214

tonynx. 2008. Blogpost in http://www.laureateci.it/forum/topic.asp?TOPIC_ID=13143 [Accessed on May 23 2013]

Torrealta, Maurizio. 2015. *La trattativa* (Milan: Rizzoli) Kindle ebook

Travaglio, M. and E. Veltri. 2001. *L'odore dei soldi* (Rome: Ed. Riuniti, 200)

Turrini, Davide. 2012. 'Venezia, applausi per Bellocchio: "Bella addormentata è l'Italia di oggi"', *Il fatto Quotidiano*, 5 September 2012 http://www.ilfattoquotidiano.it/2012/09/05/bellocchio-applausi-al-festival-di-venezia-bella-addormentata-e-litalia-di-oggi/343390/ [Accessed 23 August 2014]

Ulivi, Stefania. 2014. 'Maresco: "Belluscone, il mio film impossibile"', *Il Corriere della Sera*, 2 September http://cinema-tv.corriere.it/cinema/14_settembre_02/maresco-belluscone-mio-film-impossibile-75e30dc2-32c3-11e4-8a37-758af3cd4875.shtml [Accessed 23 December 2014]

Uva, Christian. 2012. 'L'immaginazione al potere: *Il Caimano*', in Vito Zagarrio (ed.), *Nanni Moretti. Lo sguardo morale* (Venice-Pesaro: Marsilio), pp. 231-35

Vasta, Giorgio. 2014. '"Belluscone" visto da Palermo,' *Lo straniero*, 28 October http://www.lostraniero.net/archivio-2014/169-novembre-n-173/897-belluscone-visto-da-palermo.html [Accessed 15 January 2015]

Vicinelli, Giulio. 2015. 'Maresco, "il digitale ha ucciso un'idea di cinema"', *Il Manifesto*, 30 May http://ilmanifesto.info/maresco-il-digitale-ha-ucciso-unidea-di-cinema/ [Accessed 31 May 2015]

Watters, Claire. 2011. 'Being Berlusconi: Sabbina Guzzanti's impersonation of the Italian Prime Minister between stage and screen', in V. Tsakona and D. E. Popa (ed.) *Studies in Political Humou.* (Amsterdam/Philadelphia: John Benjamins Publishing), pp. 167-90

Williams, Raymond. 1974. *Television: Technology and Cultural Form* (London: Routledge)

Wilson, Gavin. 2014. 'Cell/ular Cinema: Individuated Production, Public Sharing and Mobile Phone Film Exhibition' (unpublished doctoral dissertation, The university of Leeds; http://etheses.whiterose.ac.uk/8475/1/G.%20Wilson%20-%20Dissertaton%202.pdf [Accessed 4 May 2015])

Zucconi, Francesco. 2013. 'Il potere per le sue immagini', in *La sopravvivenza delle immagini nel cinema* (Milan-Udine: Mimesis), pp. 183-212

MIMESIS GROUP
www.mimesis-group.com

MIMESIS INTERNATIONAL
www.mimesisinternational.com
info@mimesisinternational.com

MIMESIS EDIZIONI
www.mimesisedizioni.it
mimesis@mimesisedizioni.it

ÉDITIONS MIMÉSIS
www.editionsmimesis.fr
info@editionsmimesis.fr

MIMESIS AFRICA
www.mimesisafrica.com
info@mimesisafrica.com

MIMESIS COMMUNICATION
www.mim-c.net

MIMESIS EU
www.mim-eu.com

printed by Digital Team
Fano (PU) in October 2015